Illustrated

Buick

BUYER'S GUIDE™

Cars from 1946

Richard M. Langworth

Motorbooks Internat
Publishers & Who
Osceola, Wisconsin 54020, U

First published in 1988 by Motorbooks
International Publishers & Wholesalers Inc,
PO Box 2, 729 Prospect Avenue, Osceola,
WI 54020 USA

Motorbooks International is a certified
trademark, registered with the United States
Patent Office

Printed and bound in the United States of America

The information in this book is true and complete
to the best of our knowledge. All
recommendations are made without any
guarantee on the part of the author or
publisher, who also disclaim any liability
incurred in connection with the use of this
data or specific details

We recognize that some words, model names
and designations, for example, mentioned
herein are the property of General Motors.
We use them for identification purposes only.
This is not an official publication of General
Motors

Library of Congress Cataloging-in-Publication Data
Langworth, Richard M.
    Illustrated Buick Buyer's guide.

    1. Buick automobile—Purchasing.   I. Title.
TL215.B84L37   1989   629.2′222   88-13065
ISBN 0-87938-318-6

On the front cover: Buick Gran Sport. *Jerry
Heasley*
On the back cover: A 1949 Roadmaster
convertible. *Jerry Heasley*

Motorbooks International books are also
available at discounts in bulk quantity for
industrial or sales-promotional use. For details
write to Special Sales Manager at the
Publisher's address

Contents

Preface

Buicks are cars of great character. Where else in one model could you have a Sound-sorber top with Conversation-tone quiet and a Dynaflash engine with Hi Poised Power mountings, Micropause balance, Durex bearings, Flight-weight pistons and Fireball Power? That selfsame Buick also offered Silent-zone body mountings and a Strata-flow cooling system, an Aerobat carburetor and Duomatic spark, a Resonance muffler, and Panthergaite suspension comprising Knee-action coil springs up front and Bui-coils in the rear. A Jack for Jill bumper jack was included to raise the car's Broadrim safety wheels. Drivers of 1948 Buicks were coddled with Feather-touch controls and Permi-firm steering, while they enjoyed the Sonomatic radio and warmed their feet with the Weather-Warden Venti-Heater. Safety was assured with Flashway lights, EZI mirror and Step-on brakes. Buick even promised a Whisper-Quiet rear axle—which is a bit much even for Buick fans, who are quite familiar with the notorious howler rear axles of early postwar models.

"It was guaranteed for the first fifteen feet or fifteen minutes," says Bud Juneau, chief photographer for this book, who also supplied the preceding list of 1948 trade-names. Bud's experience with early postwar Buicks is lengthy enough to warrant his remark as not quite tongue-in-cheek.

"When Better Cars Are Built, Buick Will Build Them," announced General Motors (GM), often and exuberantly. Here, any-way, was a fair slogan. Buicks *were* soundly built cars—most of them. And when Buicks were otherwise, well, so was just about everything else in the industry. In 1958, for example, big Detroit cars sold like ripe bananas, and Buick Division hit unaccustomed skids.

People have been collecting Buicks longer than they have most GM cars. Buick collecting was going strong before the first 1957 Chevy convertible started the first collector's juices flowing with its pink and gray imagery. Among recent speculative crazes that have attended everything from 1959 Cadillacs to Ferrari Daytonas, however, Buicks have been noticeably absent. Perhaps this is because of their maturity as collector cars—and the maturity of those who collect them.

This book is intended to be a comprehensive guide to the myriad collectible Buicks of the postwar era. The thirty-three chapters within cover 125 individual models, and yet this by no means exhausts the ranks of collectible postwar Buicks—which brings me to a unique feature of this book: reader participation.

After running a short list of about ninety models past the readers of *Car Collector* through my column "Postwar Cars," I received a huge outpouring of comment, critique, advice and suggestion. Two characteristics of this response point to the aforementioned maturity of Buick collectors. First, there was not a single letter from the "fever swamps," populated by the nuts of the old-car hobby, whose numbers in certain other one-make areas are legion. Second, a remarkable number of respondents admitted to a catholicity of taste that amazed me—some liked Buicks and Ferraris, for example!

Truly, Buick collectors are an advanced species. I am glad I asked for their help. Not only did I get it—but I now know twice as much as I did about collectible Buicks!

Richard M. Langworth
Hopkinton, New Hampshire

Acknowledgments

Sincere thanks are in order to Lawrence Gustin of Buick Public Relations, who is also co-author with Terry Dunham of *The Buick* —one of the best single-make histories ever published; to my long-time friend Bud Juneau; and to Bud's friend Bob Brelsford. All three of these Buick collectors and authorities read all or part of the manuscript. Bud, who is in addition a fine automotive photographer, went out to snap many of the cars you see herein; Larry Gustin kindly supplied photographic documentation for the rest.

I wish to thank equally the many people who sent me their comments, most notably those whose thoughts influenced the cars included in this book and from whom I quoted liberally: Don Allen, Victor Blakely, Jonathan Bogus, Hugo de Vries, Dennis Divine, Stephen Forristall, John T. Immesoete, Jil McIntosh, Craig N. Parslow, Jeff S. Savage, James A. Wagner and Dr. Christopher Whalley. They made writing this book fun.

From its raw state, the resulting manuscript was honed free of repetition, misspellings, clumsy phrases and plain bad English by the indefatigable Barbara Harold and Michael Dregni. Finally, the impetus for doing the job at all is owed to Publisher Tim Parker, who is one of the reasons it is always a pleasure to work for Motorbooks International. To paraphrase a circa 1940 remark by one of Tim's countrymen, never in the cause of collectible Buicks has one author owed so much to so many.

Investment rating

★★★★★ **The best Buicks** Rarely advertised, these top-value blue-chip Buicks tend to change hands quietly between private parties, mainly through word of mouth or car club contacts rather than by commercial advertising—although they are occasionally sold for high prices at auctions. They represent the top collector Buicks, with high potential for long-term appreciation. This rating has not often been applied to recent models because the values of those models have not yet settled to a point where long-term judgments can be made.

★★★★ **The next-best models** These Buicks are usually scarce or even rare models, with low original production runs. They are not easily found, but are constantly sought after by collectors and have a strong investment potential. They include most of the high-roller muscle cars like the Gran Sports, and are better short-term investments than the five-star selections. They are found often in hobby advertising, but not so often in newspapers. Auctions feature them prominently. The best sources for such cars are the Buick clubs.

★★★ **Excellent values** Buicks in reasonably good supply, though by no means common, that have demonstrated good investment value over the short to middle term are rated three stars. They are good choices for combination drivers and show cars. They may be sleepers that will move up to the high categories, in which case I have so indicated.

★★ **Good values** I like to equate these to an off-year claret: sound; well made; ready to be enjoyed right now, not set aside for future appreciation. All are reasonably priced (none should cost more than $10,000). These cars are not appreciating as rapidly as the more highly rated cars, but neither are they losing value. The odds are good that you'll be able to sell them for more than you paid for them—provided you don't overindulge in restoration.

★ **Possibilities** Speculative ventures, often including recent Buicks (which are hard to judge with any degree of finality), get one-star ratings. This rating should not dissuade you if you find a nice example and the price is right. Often these cars are too young to establish a firm state of value but they have certain characteristics of earlier Buicks that are now highly sought after. In other cases they are cars that have been on the Buick scene a long time without moving up much in value.

Common sense is more important than any rating. The best fifties Buick investment is probably the 1953 Skylark, which also costs a fortune nowadays—but the 1954 Skylark is another animal entirely, and if you don't know the difference you had better not go bidding at an auction. The 1953 Roadmaster convertible is yet another permutation, different from the Skylarks both physically and in its characteristics as a collectible Buick.

Convertibles are virtually always better investments, car for car, than are closed models, particularly two- and four-door sedans. You could almost bet on the price proportions: Whatever a convertible is worth (say, $10,000), the two-door hardtop from the same year and model is worth half that ($5,000) and the four-door sedan is worth one-fourth or one-fifth ($2,500 or $2,000). But convertibles are complicated to restore if rust has set in, and easy to botch with the wrong choice of top, upholstery materials or patterns.

Cars built over the last twenty years come from the age when Congress got into the car design business, and some 1980s models may be depreciating—officially, at least (I have not picked any lowball models among 1980s Buicks; serious Buickophiles know about things like the GNX and Riviera convertible). As usual, open models are preferable to closed, deluxe models to standard. Unique trim packages are important—pay attention to them. These recent cars are more complicated, however, with computers and fuel injection and relays galore; always try to find the mint low-mileage example rather than the handyman's special. You'll spend less in the long run.

This book does not discuss the more mundane Buicks, which tend not to be as collectible as the models noted. Most often these are four-door and two-door sedans, or nonwoody wagons, in the low-priced models. This does not mean that a 1950 Special business coupe with 500 verified "original miles" should be passed over. Common sense, the judgment born of experience, the knowledge that a mint original is worth *something* even if it's a plebian model, is what the serious collector must have. But remember: Age alone does not endow a car with any special status. If it did, that 1960 LeSabre four-door out on Route 28 wouldn't be serving as a chicken coop.

Prices

Under the Summary and prospects sections I have, when possible, listed ballpark figures for cars in excellent original or restored condition, based on known recent sales and collector opinion. Keep in mind that these are not firm figures, and prices may range both up and down from the median presented. Furthermore, the prices are for excellent cars; those in lesser condition will bring quite a bit less.

I have avoided any attempt to create lengthy lists of values in multiple categories for each model covered. I have always doubted such lists, because collector cars change hands relatively infrequently, preventing prices from being established in the same way as they are in the used-car business. Too often these lists, while handy guides, are simply made up by charting a few actual sales and filling in all the blanks around them.

More significantly, in these sections I have made judgments about whether an individual model is worth restoring, or should be bought in as pristine a condition as possible. (The last option is almost always my recommendation among Buicks of the last fifteen years.) I have also stated where, in the opinion of collectors and judging by current market trends, these cars will be priced by the year 2000.

1946-48 Roadmaster convertible

History

The Roadmaster convertible boasted a pontoon-fendered prewar body, spectacularly souped up by Buick design chief Ned Nickles, who gave it a bold, bucktooth grille; sweeping airfoil fenders, which (unlike those of the Olds or Pontiac) trailed out into the doors; and the famous gunsight hood ornament. As Buick's top-of-the-line convertible, the Roadmaster offered extro-

This magnificent 1948 Roadmaster owned by John White was traded to a Buick dealer in Lawrence, Kansas, in the 1950s, kept for light parade use and otherwise stored until 1983. It shows only 60,000 miles and is painted French gray with red leather and Bedford cord upholstery. *Bud Juneau*

A massive dashboard followed the prewar symmetrical pattern on Roadmasters through the 1948 model year, with a huge radio and speaker system in the center. Symmetry was retained even to the oblong openings to match the odometers on the speedometer. Dials were silver on the 1948. *Bud Juneau*

A good angle on these Buicks is the rear three-quarter, where Harley Earl's pontoon fenders show their sweeping length to best advantage. Pay particular attention to the correct-pattern backlight on this car's top. *Bud Juneau*

vert presence and styling that was clearly more attractive than that of its GM siblings. Many people who could afford a Cadillac preferred this luxurious Buick.

Few changes occurred to the Roadmaster in its three-year styling cycle. The established Buick engineering pattern—all-coil spring suspension, overhead-valve (ohv) straight eight—held, with the addition of Dynaflow, Buick's torque converter automatic, as a $244 Roadmaster option for 1948. Big, posh and ostentatious, the Roadmaster was the sub-Caddy answer to ego gratification in the forties.

Identification

In 1946, a Buick badge was mounted on the hood above and separate from the grille. In 1947-48, the badge with an added helmet was integrated with the grille in the center of a wing motif. In 1948, silver instrument

Buick's practical directional signal and taillight combination has the back-up light mounted horizontally outboard of the bumper guards. Some latterday retrofits have back-up lamps mounted vertically, which is more conventional but not authentic. *Bud Juneau*

A central radio antenna mounted over the windshield was a hallmark of Buicks from the early postwar years. This position was retained on the convertibles, despite their nonstandard windshield headers. Fender-mounted antennas are incorrect. *Bud Juneau*

The side-opening hood allows better access than the alligator style almost universally adopted during the 1950s, but is also conducive to paint marks and scratches if operated carelessly. *Bud Juneau*

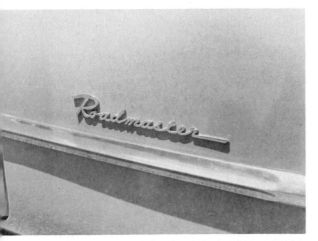

Difficult pieces to replace if missing are Roadmaster script (unique to the 1948), tunneled rear reflectors and hood corner escutcheons, which are extremely scarce as new-old-stock. Check these parts carefully when you consider an early Roadmaster. *Bud Juneau*

dials with gold numerals and a semicircular horn ring were used.

Performance and utility

Large and luxurious, this is a fine touring car but an armful to drive. It is thirsty and has sluggish pickup with the Dynaflow. It is also long enough to create parking and garage problems. Most examples leak water and dust freely.

The typical qualities of forties cars are present here: excellent fit and finish; lovely multitube radios with that "fat" sound you just don't get from transistors; and leather-swathed interiors that stand up to abuse.

Problem areas

Hydroelectric vacuum lines almost inevitably leak, causing windows to slip down in storage, allowing mice in! Keep an eye on stored cars.

Summary and prospects

These cars are good investments but are increasingly rare, and when offered, they tend to be expensive. The fastback, or sedanet, will cost less and be just as satisfying to drive, until the first warm day of spring. The convertible is the fastest-appreciating Buick of the entire period, and the Roadmaster is much more desirable than the concurrent Super convertible.

Production

	1946	1947	1948
Roadmaster convertible	2,587	12,074	11,503

1946-48 Roadmaster convertible

Engine
Type ...... eight-cylinder inline, water-cooled, cast-iron block and heads
Bore and stroke .... 3.44x4.31 in.
Displacement .... 320.2 ci
Valve operation .... overhead
Compression ratio 6.6:1
Carburetion .... dual-throat downdraft
Brake horsepower .... 144 gross @ 3600 rpm
Chassis and drivetrain
Transmission .... three-speed; Dynaflow opt.
Rear axle ratio 4.11:1
Front suspension .... independent, coil springs, lever shocks
Rear suspension ..... live axle, coil springs, lever shocks
Dimensions and weight
Wheelbase .... 129 in.
Overall length .... 217.5 in.
Track .... 59.1 in. front, 63.2 in. rear
Tire size 7.00x15 (1946-47), 8.20x15 (1948)
Curb weight .... 4315-4345 lb.
Performance
Acceleration .... 0-60 mph: 18.0 seconds
Top speed .... approx. 100 mph
Fuel mileage .... 10-14 mpg

An ornate Buick badge was integrated with the grille frame on 1947-48 models but carried separately on the hood above the grille frame on 1946 cars. This is the only significant exterior difference among the three model years. *Bud Juneau*

13

Famous Buick gunsight hood ornament was a hallmark of the early postwar cars. It is often found damaged, and replacements are scarce. *Bud Juneau*

What Larry Gustin accurately calls the pop-art grille is a traditional component. Note the mounting position of the auxiliary foglamps and the bumper guard ensemble, all parts that were standard and should be intact on Roadmasters. *Bud Juneau*

Factory artwork of the 1947 version shows an identifying item: no Roadmaster script on front fender. (Not every piece of trim in this heavily airbrushed photo is in true proportion!)

An outstanding 1948 Roadmaster convertible owned by Steve Sim Roberts (whose other love is Jaguars). "It's a complete frame-up restoration from the Blackhawk Collection. I love it! I know how the Captain of the *Queen Mary* felt," writes Steve. "Of all my cars, Jaguars included, this would be the last to go." *Steve Sim Roberts*

Chapter 2

1946-48 Super and Roadmaster estate wagons

History

Unlike sister marques such as Oldsmobile, Buick paid scant attention to station wagons before the war, putting one in the Special line only in 1941-42. After the war it was decided to work this market harder. A Super woody was available in the first 1946 model line, and a Roadmaster arrived in 1947. Both wagons were expensive, peripheral specialty models for the hotel or delivery trade or the occasional landed proprietor—hence the decision to place them in the higher-priced series rather than in the Special series.

Buick's wagons were among the few to be really styled. Thanks to the gracefully arched front and rear fenders, the white ash and

Accurate factory artwork of the 1946 model 59 Super estate wagon, showing the 1946's clear distinction: a separate Buick badge mounted on the hood independent of the grillework. The Super's wheelbase was five inches shorter than the Roadmaster's.

The 1947 Roadmaster estate wagon rode a 129 inch wheelbase, with the extra length added ahead of the cowl. The 1947 Buick badge was integrated, but Roadmaster script did not arrive until the 1948 models. These Roadmasters are the most desirable of Buick woodies, which continued as a type through the 1953 model year.

mahogany wagon body was neatly integrated to the metal underpinning, giving this woody a graceful appearance to go with its charm and character. (An incidental milestone: At $3,249, the 1946-48 Roadmaster estate wagon was the first Buick since 1921 to be base-priced at over $3,000.)

Identification

In 1946, a Buick badge was mounted on the hood above and separate from the grille. In 1947-48, the badge with an added helmet was integrated with the grille in the center of a wing motif. In 1948, silver instrument dials with gold numerals and a semicircular horn ring were used.

Performance and utility

With only 115 hp maximum, the Super was an underpowered car, anything but exciting to drive—and since its 248 straight eight was no economizer, it was not much less expensive to run than the larger Roadmaster. The Roadmaster was more lively, but weighed over two tons, which was a lot even for its huge 320 ci straight eight to push around. Dynaflow was at least theoretically available for 1948, but few of these

cars had it—and with good reason: the stick-shift helped avoid that sluggish feeling.

Utility is outstanding, with over seven feet of cargo area when the back seat is removed and eight-passenger seating when it's left in. These wagons are ideal for the swap-meet prowler who wants to arrive in style (in which case, leave the back seat at home; it doesn't fold into the floor as on 1949 and later wagons).

Problem areas

Maintenance of wooden body parts is the chief hazard with these cars. Restoration should not be undertaken; only the most dedicated expert wood surgeon should tackle badly rotted examples, and reconstruction will cost more than the resulting car will be worth.

Summary and prospects

A popular postwar woody wagon, and better looking than most of the period, the Roadmaster estate is well worth considering if you admire fine carpentry and quality materials, but good examples are by no means inexpensive and restoration is a costly undertaking. Just finding one is your hard-

In 1948, the Super estate wagon carried front fender script as well as an identifying badge mounted in the bumper guard bridge. The car was otherwise little changed from the 1947 model and continued to ride a slightly shorter wheelbase than the corresponding Roadmaster.

1946-48 Super and Roadmaster estate wagons

Engine
Type . . . . . . eight-cylinder inline, water-cooled, cast-iron block and heads
Bore and stroke . . . . . . 3.09x4.13 in. (Super), 3.44x4.31 in. (Roadmaster)
Displacement . . . 248.0 ci (Super), 320.2 ci (Roadmaster)
Valve operation . . . . overhead
Compression ratio . . . 6.3:1 (1946-47 Super), 6.6:1 (others)
Carburetion . . . . dual-throat downdraft
Brake horsepower . . . . 110 gross @ 3600 rpm (1946-47 Super), 115 gross @ 3600 rpm (1948 Super), 144 gross @ 3600 rpm (Roadmaster)

Chassis and drivetrain
Transmission . . . . three-speed; Dynaflow opt. (1948)
Rear axle ratio 4.10:1
Front suspension . . . . independent, coil springs, lever shocks
Rear suspension . . . . . live axle, coil springs, lever shocks

Dimensions and weight
Wheelbase . . . . 124 in. (Super), 129 in. (Roadmaster)
Overall length . . 212.5 in. (Super), 217.5 in. (Roadmaster)
Track . . . . 59.1 in. front, 63.2 in. rear
Tire size . . . . 6.50x16 (1946-47 Super), 7.60x15 (1948 Super), 7.00x15 (1947 Roadmaster), 8.20x15 (1948 Roadmaster)
Curb weight . . . . 4170 lb. (Super), 4445-4460 lb. (Roadmaster)

Performance
Acceleration . . . . . . 0-60 mph: 22.0 seconds (Super), 20.0 seconds (Roadmaster)
Top speed . . . . approx. 85 mph (Super), approx. 90 mph (Roadmaster)
Fuel mileage . . . . 12-15 mpg (Super), 10-14 mpg (Roadmaster)

est assignment, as the production figures suggest. The alternative is the Super version or 1949-53 models.

The Super will not appreciate quite as rapidly but is possessed of the same appeal. All that white ash and mahogany, so beautifully hung together, makes even the Super an interesting period piece. Fine examples are by far your best buy.

Outstanding Roadmaster and Super woodies are already hitting $25,000 and $20,000, respectively. Buick collectors expect that prices will be fairly static over the next few years, but it would be no surprise to see these figures double by the mid-nineties. Note also that the Roadmaster is much, much rarer; expect its price lead over the Super to increase considerably as time passes.

Production

	1946	1947	1948
Super estate wagon	748	2,036	2,018
Roadmaster estate wagon	—	529	350

★★★★	Roadmaster sedanet
★★★	Super sedanet

1949 Super and Roadmaster sedanets

History

Everybody thought the separate fender shape would go the way of the dodo after the war, but Harley Earl fooled 'em. GM Art & Colour dropped a bombshell on the industry when it brought out its first all-new postwar styling in 1948, and followed it line-wide in 1949. Sleekest and most exciting of all the sedans was the Buick sedanet, also known as the torpedo or jetback. Buick fans liked this shape so much that both variations of it are included here—but only for 1949.

The 1949 Roadmaster/Super (the Special retained 1948 styling this year) was the cleanest, purest and most lovely Buick of the new styling generation. As was often the case in those days, designers sought revision in later years by adding glitter; the 1950 Buicks saw the toothy grille extended clumsily over the bumper and the taillights less elegantly worked into the rear end.

My money is on the 1949 as the prime collectible among closed Buicks of this era, second in desirability only to the Riviera. The

Best angle on the 1949 sedanets is probably this one (Roadmaster). Though this factory illustration slightly exaggerates length and lowness, it gives an accurate feel for a design that was underrated when new. Only over the last 10 or 15 years have collectors come to appreciate this "fastback" as one of the most elegant closed Buicks of the postwar years.

Another 1949 Roadmaster sedanet, showing its true proportions. This flawless dark gray metallic example had only 18,000 miles on the odometer when the photograph was taken years ago by Roaring Twenties Autos, a collector car dealership in Wall, New Jersey.

amount of grille was just right, the fender-top parking lamps were a neat touch reminiscent of earlier days and those beautiful taillights marking the flow of the rear fenders were sheer perfection. All the 1949 needed was the 1950's sweepspear. (Though some 1949 Rivieras received the sweepspear, I have not tracked down any sedanets with it in this model year.)

Indentification

Unmistakable fastback coupe styling was used, with taillights faired into rear fenders. The grille ended above the bumper, and parking lamps were atop the fenders. Three ventiports appeared on the Super, four on the Roadmaster. The Roadmaster was noticeably longer than the Super.

Performance and utility

Drivers used to more exotic machinery will call the performance of these cars clunky and underwhelming, in part due to the Dynaflow transmission standard on the Roadmaster and almost always fitted on the Super. Nevertheless, these sedanets look so good that you can forgive them almost anything. They have plenty of room for six big passengers, with easy access to the back seat through wide doors. They also have excellent visibility for their era, but you can't see where the rear end is from the driver's seat. Fuel mileage is reasonable, better on the Super.

Problem areas

Problems are typical of those applying to early postwar Buicks.

Summary and prospects

One glance at the admiring multitude that gathers in the wake of one of these at a car

The 1949 Super sedanet had a five-inch-shorter wheelbase than the Roadmaster, and three instead of four portholes. Though the impressive lines were slightly more squeezed on this chassis, the Super offers an attractively priced alternative to the Roadmaster for the interested collector. I think it's agreed among Buick folk that the 1949 vintage is the best for this body style.

show suggests the potential they have for real value appreciation. The handwriting is already on the wall: the sedanets are well out in front of all other closed 1949s, except the Roadmaster Riviera.

Price guides, which all too often are filled in based on a tiny handful of actual prices, do not correctly reflect the sedanet's worth. They show the best-condition Roadmaster around $13,000, the best Super around $11,000, only a thousand or two ahead of the four-door sedans. Actual asking prices are near those figures; the fallacy is that the four-doors sell for much less.

While $10,000 for a coupe sounds high, it will seem almost a giveaway price in twenty years. We have seen the corresponding Cadillacs take off. There's no reason why these big, glamorous Buicks won't follow.

Production

	1949
Super sedanet	66,250
Roadmaster sedanet	18,537

1949 Super and Roadmaster sedanets
Engine
Type . . . . . . eight-cylinder inline, water-cooled, cast-iron block and heads
Bore and stroke . . . . . . 3.19x4.13 in. (Super), 3.44x4.31 in. (Roadmaster)
Displacement . . . 263.3 ci (Super), 320.2 ci (Roadmaster)
Valve operation . . . . overhead
Compression ratio . . . . 6.6:1 (Super), 6.9:1 (Roadmaster)
Carburetion . . . . dual-throat downdraft
Brake horsepower . . . . . . 115 gross @ 3600 rpm (Super), 120 gross @ 3600 rpm (Super with Dynaflow), 150 gross @ 3600 rpm (Roadmaster)
Chassis and drivetrain
Transmission . . . . three-speed (Super); Dynaflow (Roadmaster, opt. Super)
Rear axle ratio . . . . . . 4.45:1 (Super), 3.90:1 (Roadmaster)
Front suspension . . . . independent, coil springs, lever shocks
Rear suspension . . . . . live axle, coil springs, lever shocks
Dimensions and weight
Wheelbase . . . . . . 121.5 in. (Super), 126 in. (Roadmaster)
Overall length . . 209.5 in. (Super), 214.1 in. (Roadmaster)
Track . . . . 59.2 in. front, 62.2 in. rear
Tire size . . . . . . 7.60x15 (Super), 8.20x15 (Roadmaster)
Curb weight . . . . 3735 lb. (Super), 4115 lb. (Roadmaster)
Performance
Acceleration . . . . 0-60 mph: 20 seconds (Super), 17 seconds (Roadmaster)
Top speed . . . . approx. 95 mph (Super), approx. 100 mph (Roadmaster)
Fuel mileage . . . . 12-16 mpg

Chapter 4

1949-52 Roadmaster convertibles and Riviera hardtop

History

With its co-stars, Cadillac's Coupe de Ville and Oldsmobile's 98 Holiday, the Buick Riviera shares the title of first production hardtop convertible. All three were created by GM's Art & Colour Studio under Harley Earl, specifically by Ned Nickles. Buick built far more hardtops in 1949 than did either Cadillac or Oldsmobile, so the Riviera was the most popular. It cost $300 less than the Coupe de Ville but only $200 more than the

less flashy Holiday ($200 to $300 being a lot more significant then than it is now). The Riviera was in a highly competitive position versus its GM rivals.

The Riviera was designed to combine the airy feeling and luxurious interior of a convertible with the comfort of a closed sedan. Hardtops quickly proliferated, appearing in the Super line in 1950 and in the Special line in 1951. For today's collectors, however, the Roadmaster is the one to look for, with the

Initially, 1949s used a straight brightmetal spear on all models. This is factory artwork of the 1949 Roadmaster model 76C convertible, showing Flint's first all-postwar designcraft including Ned Nickles' famous portholes. A splendid Buick.

Although the first Riviera came off the line with a straight chrome molding, all those which followed—and all other body styles as well—carried the sweepspear molding, a Buick styling benchmark. This piece of art may or may not be based on the first Riviera.

Bob Brelsford's fine 1949 Roadmaster convertible shows how much improved that model was with the addition of the mid-model-year sweepspear. Nickles' styling was never better than on the smoothly integrated 1949, and the convertible is arguably the best of the lot. *Bud Juneau*

An asymmetrical dashboard was adopted with the new 1949 styling. Full pleated-leather upholstery was another feature of this top-of-the-line convertible. *Bud Juneau*

lowest production and the highest standard of luxury.

Although the Riviera hardtop has the historical significance, one could hardly omit the handsome Roadmaster convertible and its subsequent versions through the end of the straight eight era. It featured the same kind of quality materials that went into the Riviera hardtop—plus the traditional collector attraction of a convertible top. Styling was exceptional in 1949, when Buick built twice as many convertibles as Riviera hardtops. This curious inversion changed immediately, when the hardtop body style proliferated and began to sell in vast quantities from 1950 onward.

Identification

In 1949, all-new styling came forth with the first appearance of Buick's famous portholes (four on Roadmasters), and parking

Roadmasters received an extra porthole for a total of four, while the relatively plebian Supers got only three and Specials still used the prewar body in 1949. Nickles allegedly wired his portholes up with the distributor to alternately flash colored lights—how droll! *Bud Juneau*

lights were set into nacelles atop the front fenders. In 1950, grille teeth extended over the front bumper and parking lights were set into bomb-shaped bumper guards. In 1951, grille teeth receded from the bumpers and a horizontal grille bar swept down to wrap around the fenders to the wheel openings. The 1952 model was similar to the 1951 model, but chrome tailfins were added to the rear fenders.

Only one prototype was made with straight side chrome. All production Rivieras had the sweepspear, and all convertibles made after Riviera production began were sweepspear equipped. (In 1950, for the entire run, the sweepspear was extended to a number of other models, among the rarer being the Roadmaster Riviera touring sedan.)

Performance and utility

The 320 straight eight developed more power in these years, ending its career with 170 hp in 1952. In that final form it was one of the most potent straight eights in history (the postwar champion, Packard's 327, developed a high of 212 hp). Dynaflow automatic was standard on all models, and the established Buick ladder chassis, with coil springs at each corner and lever shocks, was continued. These big, roomy cars rode a 126 inch wheelbase, easily accommodating six adults and lots of cargo.

Problem areas

Rain and dust leaks are a common malady; on well-worn or improperly stored examples, replacement rubber may be necessary. Be sure to examine the little flaps that close down against the top edge of the side windows on Rivieras, for proper operation. Interior hardware is impossible to find for Rivieras—it is much easier restoring a convertible, whose top can be replicated.

Summary and prospects

With historic importance, good looks, performance and low production going for it, the early Riviera hardtop has long been a prime collector item among Buick enthusiasts. The 1949 model is a certified Milestone, worth about fifty percent more than 1950-52 models in comparable condition. (The highest reported value at this writing is $18,500.) All these Rivieras will continue to appreciate, the 1949 rising more rapidly than the later models.

With top up, a rear three-quarter view shows the correct pattern for the backlight, which is all important if a top is being replaced. Faired-in taillamps were unique to the 1949, and probably prefigured those of the 1951 Frazer. *Bud Juneau*

Bud Juneau's mint 1949 Roadmaster Riviera in yellow with a white top shows the aggressive sweepspear stance and the broadly wrapped backlight. Back-up lights were now flush-mounted and Dynaflow (see the fender script) was standard. *Bud Juneau*

The model name was proclaimed on the bumper guard connecting bar. This piece is difficult to find, easier to restore. *Bud Juneau*

With top down, the 1949 looks sensational. A car like this is a prize for the fortunate few; prices are mounting fast and survivors are scarce. *Bud Juneau*

In terms of volume, the only good year had by the Roadmaster convertible was 1949. Production in subsequent years makes those models genuine rarities, but happily this is one time that production figures are on the side of collectors: the 1949 is clearly more desirable than the rest. All are priced around the same—top dollar is now over $22,000—but the 1949 is the only one that is worth that much. All years have strong potential for future appreciation.

Production

	1949	1950	1951	1952
Riviera hardtop	4,343	2,300	13,710*	11,387
Convertible	8,244	2,964	2,911	2,402

Includes 809 models with less elaborate interior trim, manually operated windows and front seat; the rest, and all 1952s, had hydraulically operated automatic window lifts and power seats

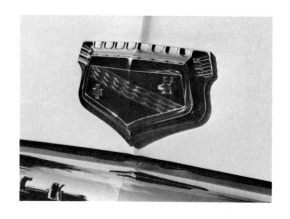

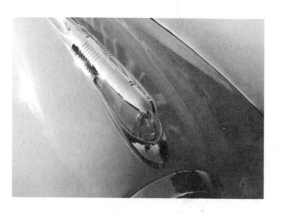

1949-52 Roadmaster Riviera hardtop
Engine
Type . . . . . . eight-cylinder inline, water-cooled, cast-iron block and heads
Bore and stroke . . . . 3.44x4.31 in.
Displacement . . . . 320.2 ci
Valve operation . . . . overhead
Compression ratio 6.9:1, 7.2:1 (1951), 7.5:1 (1952)
Carburetion . . . . 2-bbl downdraft; 4-bbl (1952)
Brake horsepower . . . . 150 gross @ 3600 rpm (1949), 152 gross @ 3600 rpm (1950-51), 170 gross @ 3800 rpm (1952)
Chassis and drivetrain
Transmission . . . . Dynaflow auto. std.
Rear axle ratio . . . . . . 3.9:1 (1949-50), 3.6:1 std. (1951-52), 3.9:1 opt. (1951-52)
Front suspension . . . . independent, coil springs, lever shocks
Rear suspension . . . . . live axle, coil springs, lever shocks
Dimensions and weight
Wheelbase . . . . 125.3 in.
Overall length . . . . . 214.5 in. (1949-50), 211 in. (1951-52)
Track . . . . 59.1 in. front, 62.4 in. rear
Tire size 8.20x15 (1949), 8.00x15 (1950-52)
Curb weight . . . . 4135-4420 lb.
Performance
Acceleration . . . 0-60 mph: 17 seconds using Lo/Hi ranges
Top speed . . . . approx. 100 mph
Fuel mileage . . . . 12-15 mpg

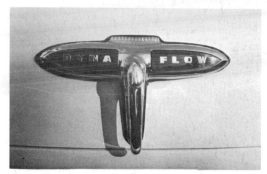

The following trim details on the 1949 should be in good order, unless you plan to pay high prices for them at swap meets (when you can find them): freestanding Buick hood badge in plastic with chrome surround, unique three-way-visible fender-mount parking lamps, and hood-mounted combination trunk handle and turn signals. Some Dynaflow cars carry turn signal lenses that read Buick Eight, but correct lenses are as the photograph shows. *Bud Juneau*

Buick's overhead-valve straight eight was a long-lived, fairly troublefree engine. Use of the correct hose clamps and the right paint finish for various underhood parts is crucial in a restoration. Everything you see here is as it should be, including the contemporary wire looms. Note hose clamp differences. *Bud Juneau*

The 1950 Buick Roadmaster Riviera was not quite as elegant as the 1949, thanks to grille teeth that were extended (not visible here) and rear fenders that were raised and had conven- tional taillights. The 1950s tend therefore to be lower priced than the 1949s, but are also not as good for investment purposes.

Commodius Roadmaster trunk houses an upright spare, with the bumper jack and lug wrench stowed inboard. Note brightmetal trim ring and size of whitewall. This factory photo should be studied when detailing the trunk compartment. *Bud Juneau*

Successive Roadmasters in 1951 and 1952 were heavier looking, but the fine original 1949 styling was by no means destroyed as it had been on certain other GM makes. This 1952 Roadmaster Riviera shows the addition of chrome fins to the rear fenders; the big housings for the round parking lights had arrived as of 1950. The 1951 model was almost identical.

This Riviera interior shows the combination Bedford cord and leather upholstery and the clever interior light, neatly faired into the C-pillar. Note also the electric window lift, and the type and application of carpeting. *Bud Juneau*

Chapter 5

★ ★ ★   **Super and Roadmaster
                              estate wagons**

1949-52 Super and Roadmaster estate wagons

History

By 1952, Buick was the only American manufacturer still offering woody wagons. Structurally, white ash figured only in the window frames and tailgate after the all-new 1949 designs. There was enough of it, however, to render the cars distinctive and desirable among collectors a generation or two later.

Both the Super and the Roadmaster continued to use straight eights in this period,

the Roadmaster having Buick's long-running 320, with 170 hp in 1952. Styling was good; among woody station wagons, these are the most highly developed in history.

Identification

In each year, the two models can be told at a glance by the number of portholes: three on the Super, four on the Roadmaster. (For general model year characteristics, see Chapter 4.)

The new-design 1949s allowed much less space for sub-beltline wooden trim. This is an early production model with the straight chrome side trim—a pretty Buick woody and not at all common (only 653 were built).

Roadmaster wagon production was even lower in 1950, when the total was 420. Like all Buicks that year, the car had grille teeth that were extended to cover the front bumper in a Niagara Falls type motif that didn't work very well. Parking lights went into large chrome-plated bombs flanking the grillework.

Performance and utility

Supers weighed about 300 pounds less than Roadmasters, but were powered by a smaller and commensurately less powerful straight eight. Dynaflow continued to remain an option on the Super, however, and many wagons are found with conventional shift, which gives much better performance and is recommended as a definite plus to the cumbersome and trouble-prone early Dynaflow.

The Roadmaster had a longer wheelbase than did the Super, but the extra inches were all forward of the cowl, so there was no difference in cargo and passenger space. The Roadmaster also had a somewhat more deluxe interior. (For more on Roadmasters, see Chapter 4.)

The Super estate wagon for 1951 had the mandatory three portholes to distinguish it from the Roadmaster. Note how the grille surround now wrapped around the front fenders. Massive woodwork was still used at the tailgate, and the back-up lamps were neatly integrated to match the front parking lamps.

Problem areas

See Chapter 2 for woody wagon problem areas (all the ones you would expect—don't let these cars stand out in the rain!).

Summary and prospects

Compared with the previous generation of prewar-designed woodies, these wagons are not appreciating as rapidly. Nevertheless, they are far more available and, as you might expect, carry much lower prices on the collector market. While ultrafine pre-1949 woodies could command as much as $25,000, the best 1949-52 example will not exceed $20,000. Despite the Roadmaster's much lower production, there is less than a $2,500 difference in typical asking prices between it and a Super in comparable condition. Prospects for both are for modest, steady gain.

Production

	1949	1950	1951	1952
Super estate wagon	1,847	2,480	2,212	1,641
Roadmaster estate wagon	653	420	679	359

1949-52 Super and Roadmaster estate wagons

Engine

Type ...... eight-cylinder inline, water-cooled, cast-iron block and heads
Bore and stroke ...... 3.19x4.13 in. (Super), 3.44x4.31 in. (Roadmaster)
Displacement ... 263.3 ci (Super), 320.2 ci (Roadmaster)
Valve operation .... overhead
Compression ratio .... 6.6:1 (1949 Super), 6.9:1 (man. Super), 7.2:1 (Dynaflow Super), 6.9:1 (1949 Roadmaster), 7.2:1 (1950-51 Roadmaster), 7.5:1 (1952 Roadmaster)
Carburetion .. 2-bbl downdraft, 4-bbl (1952 Roadmaster)
Brake horsepower .. 115 gross @ 3600 rpm (1949 Super), 120 gross @ 3600 rpm (1949 Dynaflow Super), 124 gross @ 3600 rpm (1950-52 Super), 128 gross @ 3600 rpm (1950-52 Dynaflow Super), 150 gross @ 3600 rpm (1949 Roadmaster), 152 gross @ 3600 rpm (1950-51 Roadmaster), 170 gross @ 3800 rpm (1952 Roadmaster)

Chassis and drivetrain

Transmission .... three-speed (Super); Dynaflow (Roadmaster, opt. Super)

Chassis and drivetrain

Rear axle ratio .... 4.45:1 (1949 Super), 4.10:1 (1950 Super), 3.60:1 (1951 Super), 3.90:1 opt. (1951 Super), 4.10:1 (1952 Super), 3.90:1 opt. (1952 Super), 3.90:1 (Roadmaster), 3.60:1 opt. (1951 Roadmaster)
Front suspension .... independent, coil springs, lever shocks
Rear suspension ..... live axle, coil springs, lever shocks

Dimensions and weight

Wheelbase ...... 125 in. (1949 Super), 125.5 in. (Super), 126.3 in. (Roadmaster)
Overall length .... 209.5 in. (1949-50 Super), 206.2 in. (1951-52 Super), 214.2 in. (1949-50 Roadmaster), 211.0 in. (1951-52 Roadmaster)
Track .... 59.2 in. front, 62.2 in. rear
Tire size .... 7.60x15 (Super), 8.00x15 (Roadmaster), 8.20x15 (1949 Roadmaster)
Curb weight .... 4100-4115 lb. (Super), 4470-4505 lb. (Roadmaster)

Performance

Acceleration .... 0-60 mph: approx. 20-22 seconds
Top speed .... approx. 90-95 mph
Fuel mileage .... 12-15 mpg

The 1951 Roadmaster estate wagon is quickly identified by its four portholes. Traditionally built in much lower quantities than the Super, this model saw only 679 produced—which makes it a rare sight today. Good examples are much in demand.

The last of the straight eight woody wagons were produced in 1952. Styling was almost a carbon copy of that in 1951, except that chrome tailfins were added to the rear fenders and the model names appeared in place of Dynaflow script. Super wagon production was slowing, however, and Buick built only 1,642 of these.

The final straight eight Roadmaster woody wagon, the 1952, was the scarcest of all, with a production run of only 359. It can be easily identified by its four portholes and Roadmaster rear fender script. Smooth, dished wheel covers were found mainly on Roadmasters but were also available on lesser models.

A restored Roadmaster estate wagon, owned by Bill Knudsen, seen at the West Coast Buick National in 1988. Extremely scarce, handsome and magnificently crafted, Bill's car represents one of the most desirable postwar woody wagons. *Bud Juneau*

Chapter 6

1953 Skylark

History

The first Skylark was a $5,000 limited production convertible, listed within the Roadmaster series for 1953 and referred to as such on the trunk ornament. With the comparable Cadillac Eldorado and Olds Fiesta, Skylark prefigured future GM production car features like the wraparound windshield and double sweepspear.

Compared with the standard convertible, Skylark had a lower (sectioned) body and windshield, full-open wheelwells, no venti-ports and expensive forty-spoke Borrani chrome-plated wire wheels standard. Buick

This 1953 Skylark in white with red and white upholstery is owned by Bill Knudsen. Its second owner stored the car from 1969 to 1982 and then, after some restoration work, sold the car to Knudsen in 1984. *Bud Juneau*

loaded on most conventional options as standard equipment, including tinted glass, Selectronic radio, power antenna, whitewalls and power everything.

More Skylarks were built than Eldorados and Fiestas combined. Nevertheless, the 1953 Skylark appears to have been a commemorative to mark Buick's fiftieth anniversary, since the 1954 Skylark was much less distinctive and the series was dropped in 1955. (See also Chapter 10.)

Identification

No ventiports were used. A Skylark emblem appeared on the rear fenders. A double sweepspear extended forward and back from a point on the rocker panel just ahead of the rear wheel. Chrome-plated wire wheels were standard.

Performance and utility

The Skylark had excellent performance, thanks to Buick's new ohv V-8. Although

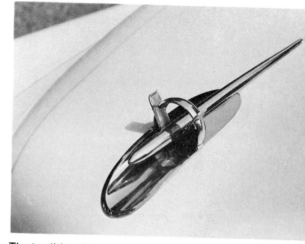

The traditional Buick hood ornament was modified in 1953 to represent the advent of the new overhead-valve V-8, Buick's first V-8. The handsome mascot was inset on the hood to visually lower the car; stylewise, this worked well. *Bud Juneau*

Lavish upholstery was a Skylark characteristic, and the amount of leather means that replacement is possible although expensive. This car's upholstery is completely original and guaranteed accurate. Door inserts under the ribbed leather use a unique tooled pattern. *Bud Juneau*

37

the V-8's horsepower was up only ten percent over the straight eight's, torque rose to a stump-pulling 300 lb-ft at 2400 rpm. Skylark 0-60 mph times were in the realm of twelve seconds, unprecedented for Buick. With the concurrent Roadmaster, the Skylark was the first big Buick capable of a 100 mph cruising speed. (Early Centurys were the first smaller Buicks to achieve 100 mph.) The power top combined with a metal boot cover to render the roof invisible when lowered.

Problem areas

Many Skylark-exclusive body parts and hardware are almost impossible to come by—and the Borrani wire wheels had better be both present and in good shape; replacements cost up to $1,200 a set. Rust began to be a significant problem with the 1953 models; Skylarks should be carefully checked for it in the floor area and trunk bottom, and up under the wheel arches, as well as throughout the rocker panels. Buick brakes were notoriously inadequate in this period; these should be carefully checked and new linings installed automatically upon purchase.

Summary and prospects

A valuable and sought-after postwar Buick, the 1953 Skylark can command close to $30,000 in absolutely pristine condition, though in practice most examples in decent shape can be had for a third less—when they

The dropped beltline unique to the Skylark (and the corresponding Cadillac Eldorado and Olds Fiesta) is clearly shown by this straight side view. This feature made the car extremely expensive to produce, and it was dropped on the 1954. *Bud Juneau*

Two sides of the new Buick V-8 are shown here to aid in accurate engine detailing. An over-square design, the 322 ci powerplant had an 8.5:1 compression ratio and produced 188 bhp at 4000 rpm. Expect yours to demand premium fuel. *Bud Juneau*

1953 Skylark

Engine
Type ..... eight-cylinder V-type, water-cooled, cast-iron block and heads
Bore and stroke .... 4.00x3.20 in.
Displacement .... 322.0 ci
Valve operation .... overhead
Compression ratio 8.5:1
Carburetion .... 4-bbl downdraft
Brake horsepower .... 188 gross @ 4000 rpm

Chassis and drivetrain
Transmission .... Dynaflow std.
Rear axle ratio 3.60:1
Front suspension .... independent, coil springs, lever shocks (1953), tube shocks (1954)
Rear suspension ..... live axle, coil springs, lever shocks

Dimensions and weight
Wheelbase .... 121.5 in.
Overall length .... 211.6 in.
Track .... 60 in. front, 62 in. rear
Tire size 8.00x15
Curb weight .... 4315 lb.

Performance
Acceleration .... 0-60 mph: 12.0 seconds
Top speed .... approx. 105 mph
Fuel mileage .... 12-18 mpg

change hands, which they rarely do. When *Special Interest Autos* tested one some seventeen years ago, it pegged the car's top value at only $2,010, meaning that the Skylark has enjoyed an annual appreciation of over eighty percent. It is doubtful that this level will be sustained, but on the other hand, the year 2000 ought to see these cars at $125,000, which sounds phenomenal today. This is one example of a car worth restoring whatever its condition.

Production

	1953
Skylark	1,690

Skylark's rakish double sweepspear and dropped beltline are shown off to particular advantage from this angle. There is no mistaking this car for any other Buick. Certainly this is a five-star investment, now and for the foreseeable future. *Bud Juneau*

40

Chrome-plated Kelsey-Hayes wire wheels were standard on the Skylark and can be counted on to give trouble if encountered in anything short of perfect condition. Spokes should be checked individually for soundness; balancing must be done by a sympathetic hand. *Bud Juneau*

Skylark badges are located ahead of the rear wheelwells in the V formed by the sweepspears. Badges are unique to the Skylark, and ought to be intact. Spears are flatter than on conventional Buicks, and again Skylark-only. These trim bits make improvements a challenge, but the results are worth it. *Bud Juneau*

The Skylark had four colors of ribbed-leather upholstery. Full leather upholstery consists of plain bolsters and pleated inserts in contrasting colors. Leather can be replaced, but is expensive. (Leather should never be replaced with vinyl, which will lower a car's value.) The front bench moves forward automatically when the backrest is tilted. *Bud Juneau*

1953-54 Roadmaster convertible and Riviera hardtop

Engine

Type ..... eight-cylinder V-type, water-cooled, cast-iron block and heads
Bore and stroke .... 4.00x3.20 in.
Displacement .... 322.0 ci
Valve operation .... overhead
Compression ratio 8.5:1
Carburetion .... 4-bbl downdraft
Brake horsepower .... 188 gross @ 4000 rpm

Chassis and drivetrain

Transmission .... Dynaflow auto.
Rear axle ratio 3.60:1
Front suspension .... independent, coil springs, lever shocks
Rear suspension ..... live axle, coil springs, lever shocks

Dimensions and weight

Wheelbase .... 121.5 in.
Overall length .... 207.6 in.
Track .... 60 in. front, 62.2 in. rear
Tire size 8.00x15
Curb weight .... 4125 lb.

Performance

Acceleration .... 0-60 mph: approx. 13.0 seconds
Top speed .... 110 mph
Fuel mileage .... 12-15 mpg

world should not cost $20,000, and a Riviera in ninety-five-point condition will sell for half that. Buy the nicest example you can find, because it is easy to overspend the car's ultimate value on a restoration.

Production

	1953
Roadmaster convertible	3,318
Riviera hardtop	22,927

1953 Super and Roadmaster estate wagons

History

The 1953 Buick woody wagon was the last of this interesting breed produced by any American manufacturer. Conversely, it was the first Buick woody with a V-8. The northern ash framing and mahogany insert panels were, as before, nicely integrated with the all-steel roof and steel lower body, and the 1953's handsome front end added to their allure. Inside, tailgate panels were finished

This stunning 1953 Roadmaster estate wagon, painted Victoria maroon with a gray and burgundy interior, is owned by the Ramshead Car Collection, Sacramento, California. The car underwent a ground-up restoration beginning in 1980 and ending in 1985. *Bud Juneau*

47

Buick built 670 of this model, but attrition has been heavy, and fewer than 15 are known to exist. Together with its Super line mate, this car represents the last series-production woody wagon built in America: a historic collector item. *Bud Juneau*

Quadruple portholes again signify the Roadmaster series. Porthole design was different in 1953, as were the wheel covers with a prominent V motif to help emphasize the powerful new 322 V-8, which gave the wagon plenty of hauling power. *Bud Juneau*

in birch, with metal runners; carpeting was hard-wearing Roxpoint nylon; and seats in both models were of genuine leather.

Identification

A vertical-tooth grille was used; parking lights moved into oval nacelles under the headlamps; and rear fenders were raised, squared off and given twin cone-shaped taillights mounted vertically on either side of a small reflector. The Roadmaster carried four ventiports, the Super three.

Performance and utility

Both the Super and the Roadmaster enjoyed the modern, oversquare 322 ci Buick V-8 in 1953, but Supers had lower compression and two-barrel instead of four-barrel carburetors, yielding 164 hp with stickshift or 170 hp with optional Dynaflow. Roadmasters came with 188 hp, Dynaflow and power steering as standard. The best-

performing woody wagons, with undeniable quality and craftsmanship, were a fitting end to a traditional body style.

Problem areas

The usual problems (listed in earlier chapters) as regards wooden body structure are present here. It is essential to keep woodies indoors in wet weather; moisture permeating the varnish will soon work into joints and spread—followed by rot. It is possible to bleach and to partly replace affected areas, but expert advice should be sought from fellow woody owners and restoration professionals. Check all steel body areas for rust.

Summary and prospects

Although more desirable from a styling and performance standpoint than any previous woody, neither the Roadmaster nor the Super has yet exceeded the $20,000

The dashboard of the Ramshead Collection's Roadmaster woody is that of a conventional 1953 Roadmaster. Just visible on the steering wheel hub is the red, white and blue Buick 50th anniversary emblem. Note the two styles of pleated upholstery on the door panels. *Bud Juneau*

mark as absolute top dollar, and some examples have sold for half that or less. As with all woody wagons, condition is crucial, for it is difficult and expensive to restore deteriorated structural wood. These V-8 models probably stand to appreciate somewhat faster than their straight-eight predecessors of the 1949-52 period.

Production

	1953
Super estate wagon	1,830
Roadmaster estate wagon	670

The tailgate structure is entirely of white ash and traditional in proportion, although set at a fairly rakish angle. Wood condition is the most crucial factor when judging the worth of these woodies, but the cars are so rare that a total restoration may be warranted. *Bud Juneau*

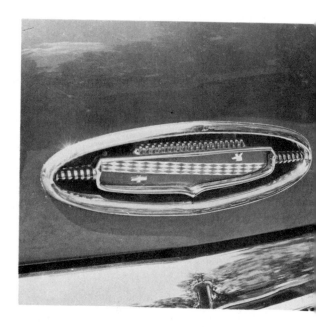

Buick's back end escutcheon carries the Road-master name under the circle and V motif. Though unique in its 1953 shape, this bauble is a throwback to the earliest postwar Buicks (clever designers came up with the V between Buick and Eight). *Bud Juneau*

Floating-style hood ornament was a feature of the 1953 line; replacements are as hard to find as you'd imagine. *Bud Juneau*

The 1953 Super estate wagon had about three times as much volume as the scarce Roadmaster. A five-inch-shorter wheelbase makes the Super look rather chunky, and the car still has but three portholes. Supers are not hitting the price levels of Roadmasters, but supplies point to strong collector demand for the junior model as well, in future years.

1953 Super and Roadmaster estate wagons

Engine
Type ..... eight-cylinder V-type, water-cooled, cast-iron block and heads
Bore and stroke .... 4.00x3.20 in.
Displacement .... 322.0 ci
Valve operation .... overhead
Compression ratio .... 8.0:1 (Super), 8.5:1 (Roadmaster)
Carburetion .... 2-bbl downdraft (Super), 4-bbl (Roadmaster)
Brake horsepower ...... 164 gross @ 4000 rpm (Super), 170 gross @ 4000 rpm (Dynaflow Super), 188 gross @ 4000 rpm (Roadmaster)

Chassis and drivetrain
Transmission .... Dynaflow (three-speed opt. on Super)
Rear axle ratio 3.60:1
Front suspension .... independent, coil springs, tube shocks
Rear suspension ..... live axle, coil springs, lever shocks

Dimensions and weight
Wheelbase .... 121.5 in.
Overall length .... 207.6 in.
Track .... 60 in. front, 62 in. rear
Tire size .... 7.60x15 (Super), 8.00x15 (Roadmaster)
Curb weight .... 4150 lb. (Super), 4315 lb. (Roadmaster)

Performance
Acceleration .... 0-60 mph: 15.0 seconds
Top speed .... approx. 100 mph
Fuel mileage .... 11-15 mpg

Chapter 9

1954 Skylark

History

Making another stab at the limited-edition market in 1954, but with much less enthusiasm, the Skylark was afterward discontinued, although its name later reappeared on a sixties compact. Compared with the unique 1953 model, the 1954 was much more conventional despite being listed as a separate Series 100 model in its own right. It shared the short-wheelbase Special-Century body, and it boasted the big, 200 hp Century engine, which gave it excellent performance.

Although the 1954 Skylark was priced some $500 below the 1953 Skylark, fewer than 1,000 1954s were sold, possibly be-

Factory artwork shows the 1954 Skylark, a more conventional successor to the 1953 version. Visible here is the "rich genuine leather in colors chosen to harmonize with body finish, attractively two-toned by darker block-embossed leather inserts on cushions and seatbacks."

A 1954 Skylark at the Buick West Coast National, 1988, whose owner was not available. This angle shows the 1954's more conventional lower body, with the characteristic, rakish double sweepspear. Although the front end looks very conventional, anyone remotely knowledgeable will know the 1954 Skylark at a glance. *Bud Juneau*

Chrome-plated wire wheels remained part of the Skylark package in 1954. The emblem, located in the "V" between the two sweepspears, was unique to the model and is almost impossible to find loose. Note also the extended rear portion of the large open wheelwells; this area was sometimes painted red by the factory. *Bud Juneau*

cause there was little noticeable difference from conventional convertibles priced about $1,000 less. Unlike the 1953's body the 1954's was not sectioned, but the huge chrome-plated taillight fins were unique. The most interesting new touch was an elongated style of wheel opening—oval in shape, tapering back well beyond the wheel centers.

Identification

Model identification appeared on the deck lid and on the lower body sides just ahead of the rear wheel cutouts. Kelsey-Hayes wire wheels were standard.

Performance and utility

Along with the Century (the best-performing Buick in the 1954 line), the Skylark gave a 0-60 time of twelve seconds or less and an honest 100 mph, eighteen-second quarter-mile. It had ample room for six big passengers, and Dynaflow and power steering were standard.

Problem areas

This is another Buick plagued with hard-to-find body hardware—the chrome-plated tailfins are impossible to locate. Check for rust, and have an expert mechanic (if you aren't one yourself) go over the engine. The Dynaflow is prone to leakage, although not as much so as with earlier models.

Summary and prospects

The 1954 Skylark is certainly a desirable postwar Buick, but not quite in the five-star category of the 1953 Skylark. Price guides show top-condition 1954s around the $20,000 mark, about $7,500 less than the best 1953s, despite the relative scarcity of the later model.

The most distinctive part of the 1954 was its tail end, where two enormous, chrome-plated tailfins sprouted, containing the large, raked taillights. Note also the deck lid ridges culminating in small chrome spacers between the deck and bumper guards, and the special back-up lights —there is nothing back here common to the workaday 1954 Buick. *Bud Juneau*

From lower down, the 1954 Skylark looks its best. Headlamp surrounds and the vertical-bar grille came from the XP-300 show car, and also showed up the very same year on the 1954 Kaiser. (President Edgar Kaiser so admired the XP-300 that he asked for a similar front end, not realizing that Buick itself was bringing out a similar design for the same year! But so few Kaisers were built that Buick did not protest.) *Bud Juneau*

1954 Skylark

Engine
Type . . . . . eight-cylinder V-type, water-cooled, cast-iron block and heads
Bore and stroke . . . . 4.00x3.20 in.
Displacement . . . . 322.0 ci
Valve operation . . . . overhead
Compression ratio 8.5:1
Carburetion . . . . 4-bbl downdraft
Brake horsepower . . . . 200 gross @ 4100 rpm

Chassis and drivetrain
Transmission . . . . Dynaflow
Rear axle ratio 3.40:1
Front suspension . . . . independent, coil springs, tube shocks
Rear suspension . . . . . live axle, coil springs, lever shocks

Dimensions and weight
Wheelbase . . . . 122 in.
Overall length . . . . 206.3 in.
Track . . . . 59 in. front, 59 in. rear
Tire size 7.60x15
Curb weight . . . . 4260 lb.

Performance
Acceleration . . . . 0-60 mph: 12.0 seconds
Top speed . . . . approx. 105 mph
Fuel mileage . . . . 12-18 mpg

Production

	1954
Skylark	836

Chapter 10

1954-56 Century convertible and Riviera hardtops

History

Salespeople touted it as "our hot rod," and not without veracity. The 1954-56 Century was to Buick as the 1949 88 had been to Oldsmobile: a big-car engine in a middle-sized body, delivering Performance with a capital *P*, the quickest model in the line.

The 1953 anomaly that had seen the Roadmaster on the same wheelbase as lesser models ended in 1954, when both the Road-master and the Super went to 127 inches, and the Century used the Special body and 122 inch wheelbase. You paid $200 to $300 more for the Century than for the comparable Special, and got a genuine 100 mph cruiser, able to leap to sixty in under twelve seconds if you pushed hard enough. Acceleration was brisker if you settled for the standard stickshift rather than the Dynaflow ($150 extra on the Century).

Stylewise, the 1954 Century Riviera was not particularly well thought of in its day. Lately, however, it has become a favorite of Buick fans and a fast-rising collectible. The front end was based on the XP-300 show car, which also influenced the design of the 1954 Kaiser. Fortunately, there weren't enough Kaisers to worry Flint.

Buick's hot Riviera in its 1955 form had the vertical-bar grille finally abandoned and the modest twin taillights replaced by a huge vertical housing. Note the porthole count: the Special was the only Buick with fewer than four in 1955.

Despite bulk, the Century was reasonably styled, and put together with a precision that later Buicks lacked. Although sedans and wagons were offered in the 1954-55 lines, Century's success was built around the sportier models and the new four-door Riviera hardtop of 1955-56.

Identification

Century nameplates appeared on the rear fenders in all three years. In 1954, narrow vertical grille teeth were used; in 1955, a grid-type grille appeared, with a chrome bar containing the Buick emblem; in 1956, a small mesh grille was used, with a large winged circular emblem (containing, of all things, the digits 1956). Centurys received four ventiports in 1955 and 1956.

Performance and utility

These cars had outstanding performance in all three years, thanks to the potent 322 V-8. The Century was the only short-wheelbase Buick offering this engine, which had the same power as the Super and Roadmaster: 200 to 255 hp. Dynaflow became standard in 1956, so Buick fans interested in maximum performance will want to look for

A fine mesh grille and teardrop portholes marked the 1956 Century convertible. The gunsight hood ornament had departed in favor of a short-lived aircraftlike affair. Fewer than 5,000 of this model were built, and it is a particularly scarce car today.

The large round grille medallions of 1956 Buicks contained the model year date—a practice frowned upon by dealer and customer alike in those model-year-conscious days, and soon eliminated. This is the Riviera version of the 1956 Century.

This beautifully prepared, mostly original 1955 Century convertible owned by Don Miller was finished in light blue and cream with a dark blue interior. Options included wire wheels, a popular item in 1955. *Bud Juneau*

1954-55 models with three-speed manual shifters—which are not, however, easy to find. Most common of the pillarless Centurys is the interesting four-door Riviera, which was outselling the convertible and two-door Riviera combined by 1956.

Problem areas

A sturdy, long-lived car, the Century's main problem was that many cars were abused, thanks to the performance it was constantly tempting contemporary owners to use. Prospective purchases should have a clean bill of health in the engine, transmission and drivetrain departments. Also check for rust and for cracks or holes in the exhaust system, and pay special attention to the brake linings and front-end alignment.

Summary and prospects

These Centurys are a good investment, not forbiddingly priced at present but probably destined to move up in value quite rapidly in the nineties. The finest Century convertible in the world should not cost more than $17,500, and comparable hardtops bring $10,000 less. The more gaudy, Dynaflow-only 1956 models command ten percent less, car for car, than do the 1954-55s.

My money is on the 1954 convertible as the best buy: cleanest styling, topless motoring—a heady combination. *The Buick* co-author Larry Gustin writes: "In its day, the '54 was considered to be breathtakingly beautiful, somehow much sharper and modern than the more rounded earlier models. The styling seemed more different then than it does now, when I look at the photos. Still, I think you are right, the '54 is the best looking of those years—though from today's perspective the '53s, with their more massive grille, seem to be more classical Buick."

Production

	1954	1955	1956
Century convertible	2,790	5,588	4,721
Riviera two-door hardtop	45,710	80,338	33,334
Riviera four-door hardtop	—	55,088	55,973

On that odometer were 75,592 miles at the time this car was photographed. The Century spent most of its life in Grass Valley, California, and was purchased by Miller in 1975. *Bud Juneau*

1954-56 Century convertible and Riviera hardtops

Engine
Type . . . . . eight-cylinder V-type, water-cooled, cast-iron block and heads
Bore and stroke . . . . 4.00x3.20 in.
Displacement . . . . 322.0 ci
Valve operation . . . . overhead
Compression ratio . . . . 8.0:1, 8.5:1 (Dynaflow)
Carburetion . . . . 4-bbl downdraft
Brake horsepower . . . . 195 gross @ 4100 rpm (1954), 200 gross @ 4100 rpm (1954 Dynaflow), 236 gross @ 4600 rpm (1955), 220 gross @ 4400 rpm (1956)

Chassis and drivetrain
Transmission . . . . . three-speed; Dynaflow (opt. 1954-55, std. 1956)

Chassis and drivetrain
Rear axle ratio 3.40:1 (1954-55), 3.36:1 (1956)
Front suspension . . . . independent, coil springs, tube shocks
Rear suspension . . . . . live axle, coil springs, lever shocks (1954-55), tube shocks (1956)

Dimensions and weight
Wheelbase . . . . 122 in.
Overall length . . . . . . 206.5 in. (1954-55), 205.1 in. (1956)
Track . . . . 59 in. front, 59 in. rear
Tire size 7.60x15
Curb weight . . . . 3795-4045 lb.

Performance
Acceleration . . . . 0-60 mph: 10-12 seconds
Top speed . . . . approx. 105-110 mph
Fuel mileage . . . . 13-18 mpg

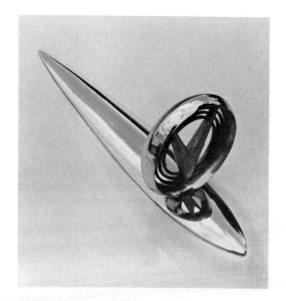

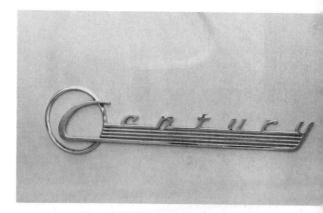

Some details of the 1955's distinctive styling are shown here. The gunsight hood ornament continued to employ the V motif, and a traditional badge was used out back—but there was nothing like the big, bold taillights that had been seen around Flint before. *Bud Juneau*

With its top up, the Century displays the broad backlight used on convertibles for 1955 and the several preceding years. *Bud Juneau*

The porthole design changed again in 1955. *Bud Juneau*

1955-56 Special convertible and Riviera hardtops

History

The Buick Special toppled Plymouth from its traditional number-three sales position in 1955, despite a price bracket more than $300 above the Plymouth level. The Special's big sales gun that year was not its four-door sedan, as you might expect, but its two-door hardtop Riviera.

Special Riviera two-doors had been around since 1952 and had matched four-doors in sales in 1954, but for 1955 Buick sold over 150,000 of them, against little more than half as many four-doors. And the company sold 66,000 four-door Special Rivieras to boot.

The key to this model's newfound popularity was its standard-equipment V-8 engine, a 1954 development that gave it tremendous appeal during the horsepower-mad mid-fifties. With V-8 performance came luxury and high-stepping good looks, a combination that was hard to beat. Styling

If you can't afford (or find) a Century convertible, what about a 1955 Special? Buick built twice as many Specials as Centurys, and the Special is almost as much car as the glamorous Century.

was big and brash, purposely close to that of the more expensive Supers and Roadmasters, although Specials shared a shorter wheelbase with the Century.

The 1956 edition received only a slight facelift. Although industry sales were off considerably that year, Buick still managed to sell over 200,000 Rivieras.

Identification

In 1955, a grid-pattern grille with center medallion and circular parking lights were used. In 1956, a thinner-grid grille appeared. Both years had Special script on rear fender or doors and only three ventiports (the Century, sharing the same wheelbase, had four).

Performance and utility

An excellent performer with Dynaflow, which was optional but usually fitted, the Special will not run with the hotter Century but is more than adequate for modern highway speeds. Dynaflow models had a higher rear axle ratio than did manual cars.

These cars had excellent quality of materials, and fit and finish, plentiful room for six full-size passengers, reasonable fuel economy and drivability. Standard back-up

lights, directional signals, front and rear pull-down armrests, and tubeless tires make the Special appealing to modern-day collectors who want a road-ready hobby car.

Problem areas

The dreaded tinworm rears its ugly head inside fenderwells, and its presence in the floor pan is made known by the famous phenomenon of rising floor mats. Engines are strong, but automatic transmissions have been known to give problems.

The Special is less desirable than the Century—and the 1954 Special model is not worth mentioning. The drill here is to look for an ultraclean, low-mileage example and avoid a lot of expensive headaches.
pensive headaches.

Summary and prospects

The 1954-56 Special is not a great Buick investment, but popular through its sheer numbers. Buick built almost half a million Riviera hardtops and a relatively large number of convertibles, which means there is a good variety of survivors to choose from.

Never destined for blue-chip status, this is nevertheless a highly satisfying car to own, happily available for a reasonable amount of money. A good convertible can

Here is a good view of the interior detailing on the 1956 Special convertible. In both 1955 and 1956, production was around 10,000. Both cars, but the 1956 especially, can still be found in fine condition for under $10,000 (these are among the few convertibles from the middle to late 1950s about which you can still say that).

still be found for under $10,000, and Riviera hardtops in prime condition cost as little as $5,000 (four-door) or $7,000 (two-door).

Production

	1955	1956
Century convertible	10,009	9,712
Riviera two-door hardtop	155,818	113,861
Riviera four-door hardtop	66,409	91,025

1954-56 Special convertible and Riviera hardtops

Engine

Type ..... eight-cylinder V-type, water-cooled, cast-iron block and heads
Bore and stroke .... 3.63x3.20 in., 4.00x3.20 in. (1956)
Displacement .... 264 ci (1954-55), 322 ci (1956)
Valve operation .... overhead
Compression ratio ... 7.2:1 (1954), 8.1:1 (1954 Dynaflow), 8.4:1 (1955), 8.9:1 (1956)
Carburetion .... 2-bbl downdraft
Brake horsepower .... 143 gross @ 4200 rpm (1954), 150 gross @ 4200 rpm (1954 Dynaflow), 188 gross @ 4800 rpm (1955), 220 gross @ 4400 rpm (1956)

Chassis and drivetrain

Transmission .... three-speed; Dynaflow opt.
Rear axle ratio ...... 3.9:1, 3.6:1 (Dynaflow), 3.2:1 (1956)
Front suspension .... independent, coil springs, tube shocks
Rear suspension ..... live axle, coil springs, lever shocks (1954-55), tube shocks (1956)

Dimensions and weight

Wheelbase .... 122 in.
Overall length .... 205-207 in.
Track .... 59 in. front, 59 in. rear
Tire size 7.60x15 (1954-55), 7.10x15 (1956)
Curb weight .... 3720-3880 lb.

Performance

Acceleration .... 0-60 mph: 12-13 seconds
Top speed .... approx. 100-105 mph
Fuel mileage .... 13-20 mpg

1957-58 Century convertible, Riviera hardtops and Caballero wagon

History

The 1957-58 Century was a continuation of an established pattern: a hotter Buick engine in the lightest Buick Special body, still only 122 inches of wheelbase but a lot more powerful. In 1957, Buick switched over en masse to a larger and improved V-8. But, whereas the Special's two-barrel unit developed only 250 hp, the Century (and Super-Riviera) engine came with a four-barrel carb and 300 hp as standard—and a power pack option giving 330 hp for a truly smoking model. Although heavier than the 1956 models, these later Centurys were much quicker off the mark, making them the most rapid Buicks in the 1957-58 line, and in history.

For 1957, styling was a straightforward evolution of the 1956 look. For 1958, however, it was considerably hammed up with a gaudy grille and heavy chrome ornamentation plus, of course, tailfins.

Partly as a result of styling, but mainly owing to the 1958 recession, sales slipped

Styling of the 1957 Buicks was traditional, with a strong resemblance to that for cars of the recent past, and model for model, collectors prefer 1957s to 1958s. Thus, the 1957 Century convertible is the most desirable car in this chapter. Note the superstreamlined portholes and the interesting red stripe on the sweepspear.

A less expensive alternative to the convertible, the 1957 Century Riviera four-door had the largest production volume of the six models in this chapter. Two-tone paint jobs were common. The least popular design feature of the Riviera was the backlight pillars, dividing the rear window into three parts. The model name remained on the grille medallion for 1957.

badly in 1958. Buick ran fourth behind Plymouth in both 1957 and 1958. (See also notes on the Caballero in the appendix entitled Comments from Buick collectors.)

Identification

Century nameplate and four ventiports (oval in shape) distinguished the 1957 models from the Specials. The name appeared again within rear fender flashes and also on the deck for 1958, when all Buicks received flashy grilles composed of 160 chrome-plated squares, and quad headlamps.

Also unique on the 1957 were rear window struts, bisecting the backlight into a main section flanked by quarter-lights. Ru-mor had it that GM was trying to get the public used to this look in order to cantilever car roofs, eliminating the A-pillars—witness Virgil Exner's Norseman show car for Chrysler in this same period. In any case, the public looked askance at the trisected backlight.

Performance and utility

Weight was up by almost 200 pounds in 1957 and by another 150 in 1958. The 1958s were clumsy beasts, plungers on curves and rippled surfaces, and withal quite a handful. Dynaflow, by then standard on Centurys, was unavoidable. These cars had a high fuel thirst, especially in 1958, and their quality of finish was not up to pre-

The Century changed dramatically, and most say for the worse, with a gaudy 1958 facelift. Convertibles like this are selling for around $12,000 in 95 point condition, against up to $18,000 for 1957 Century convertibles.

proximate condition. Valuewise, the 1957 models are on the same level as their 1955-56 counterparts, while the 1958s are commensurately lower priced. Still, the exceptional low-mileage 1958 may be preferred by some to a 1957 needing restoration. Buicks became increasingly complex in this period, and are as a result more difficult and more expensive to restore than are examples from the early fifties.

"Off the record," says one Buick authority, "the '58 to me looks so bad I'm not sure I'd take a nice '58 to a rough '57. The '57 had ugly rear window pillars, but still had classic Buick vestiges: portholes, sweep-spear, vertical grille."

Production

	1957	1958
Century convertible	4,085	2,588
Riviera two-door hardtop	17,029	8,100
Riviera four-door hardtop	26,589	15,171

1957-58 Century convertible and Riviera hardtops

Engine

Type . . . . . eight-cylinder V-type, water-cooled, cast-iron block and heads
Bore and stroke . . . . 4.13x3.40 in.
Displacement . . . . 364.0 ci
Valve operation . . . . overhead
Compression ratio 10.0:1
Carburetion . . . . 4-bbl downdraft
Brake horsepower . . . . 300 gross @ 4600 rpm

Chassis and drivetrain

Transmission . . . . Dynaflow
Rear axle ratio 3.58:1 (1957), 3.23:1 (1958)
Front suspension . . . . independent, coil springs, tube shocks, ball joints (new in 1957)
Rear suspension . . . . . live axle, coil springs, tube shocks
Optional suspension . . . . air bag four-wheel (1958)

Dimensions and weight

Wheelbase . . . . 122 in.
Overall length . . . . 208.4 in. (1957), 211.8 in. (1958)
Track . . . . 59.5 in. front, 59 in. rear
Tire size 7.60x15
Curb weight . . . . 4081-4302 lb.

Performance

Acceleration . . . . 0-60 mph: 10-11 seconds
Top speed . . . . 115 mph
Fuel mileage . . . . 13-18 mpg

Chapter 13

1958 Limited

History

To understand the Limited, one has to bear in mind the three-year gestation period of the typical new Detroit model. Given that the 1958s were planned in 1955—which marked a high point in consumer demand for chrome and flash—the Limited's arrival in small-car-minded 1958 is comprehensible.

Unfortunately, that brought it smack up against a recession year in which the only significant sales gains were by Rambler and Volkswagen.

Long dismissed as a monument to excess, the Limited was more importantly an attempt to revive an old top-of-the-line series. Carefully priced a few hundred dollars be-

The 1958 Series 75 Limited four-door Riviera is depicted here in a piece of factory artwork—stretched somewhat, but clearly showing the range of conflicting baubles attached to the top of the 1958 line from stem to stern. To col-

lectors with a sense of fun, the Limited represents an inverse snob appeal: it's *so* bad that it endears itself to you. Subjectively, it's a kind of VW Beetle at the other end of the scale.

The most collectible of Limiteds is of course the convertible, though this brightly overdecorated chrome-wagon hasn't yet taken off on the auction circuit at the levels of the equally garish 1959 Cadillac. It's tailfins that count in the auction league; still, if you want glitter, this Buick provides it.

low comparable Cadillac Sixty-Two models, it seemed like a sensible idea in 1955—but then again, so did the Edsel. Today the Limited represents all the worst styling excesses of the fifties but, at the same time, a sort of reverse snob appeal. (A Detroit stylist used to commute to work in a pink Limited convertible, embarrassing everyone who shared the parking lot at the [Ford!] Design Center, where he crafted slick aerodynamic shapes for the eighties.)

The worst possible year for a car of its type was 1958, and the Limited sold in quantities befitting its name; it was lopped off the model list the following year. Its departure was almost simultaneous with that of Edward T. Ragsdale (Buick's manufacturing manager from 1949 to 1956 and general manager from 1956 to 1959), who had tried to keep Buick out of rags and in riches.

To a large extent Ragsdale, like many others, was a victim of a dramatic shift in public attitudes toward cars. And one can't write him off completely: he was, after all, responsible for the cleanly styled, newly named Buick LeSabre, Invicta and Electra of 1959. And he had a hand in the development of the 1949 Riviera hardtop convertible—his wife Sarah may even have sparked the whole thing when she let on that she liked convertibles but didn't enjoy the way they mussed her hairdos.

Identification

These cars displayed twelve forward-raked vertical dummy louvers on the rear fenders, special louvered taillights and Limited script on the rear doors or quarters. They had very posh interiors combining cloth and leather, with full leather upholstery on convertibles.

Performance and utility

Slow and ponderous despite its 300 hp, the Limited exceeded two tons curb weight and had a notorious thirst for high-test gasoline. Although this car was smooth and comfortable on the highway, hard work was needed to drive it around town. There is no bigger or flashier example of 1958 American luxury boats, save perhaps the concurrent Cadillac Eldorado.

Problem areas

Limited-only body parts are in short supply or unobtainable, and these cars were rust-prone. Restoration of the elaborate interiors poses the most serious challenges. Some parts may have to be fabricated. A low-mileage original example is strongly recommended, since it is quite easy to over-invest in a restoration, leaving you with a car worth much less than you have in it.

A relatively high proportion of these cars originally had Buick's Cadillac-based optional air suspension, but many have since had this replaced with more reliable stock coil springs. A high compression ratio means this car is unhappy with most grades of gas available today (see notes under Problem areas in Chapter 12).

Summary and prospects

The Limited commands a higher price on today's market than do lesser 1958 Buicks (one rather optimistic value guide giving $17,000 for a ninety-point convertible). This is entirely relative, however; remember that 1957 Centurys, for example, are much more desirable than 1958 Centurys. The exceptionally fine low-mileage convertible may command $15,000, but in practice most Limiteds—even some convertibles—sell for $4,000 to $7,000.

I believe appreciation is likely to be low, even with inflation. To this, long-time Buick collector Bud Juneau says: "I disagree. My collector sense tells me the convertible Limited will go up quite well, a la '59 Cadillacs, which are going like wildfire right now. Perhaps it won't rise geometrically, but it will increase steadily over the years."

Production

	1958
Limited convertible	839
Riviera two-door hardtop	1,026
Riviera four-door hardtop	5,571

1958 Limited

Engine
Type ..... eight-cylinder V-type, water-cooled, cast-iron block and heads
Bore and stroke .... 4.13x3.40 in.
Displacement .... 364.0 ci
Valve operation .... overhead
Compression ratio 10.0:1
Carburetion .... 4-bbl downdraft
Brake horsepower .... 300 gross @ 4600 rpm
Chassis and drivetrain
Transmission .... Dynaflow
Rear axle ratio 3.23:1
Front suspension .... independent, coil springs, tube shocks

Chassis and drivetrain
Rear suspension ..... live axle, coil springs, tube shocks
Optional suspension .... air bag four-wheel
Dimensions and weight
Wheelbase .... 127.5 in.
Overall length .... 227.1 in.
Track .... 60 in. front, 61 in. rear
Tire size 8.00x15
Curb weight .... 4603-4710 lb.
Performance
Acceleration .... 0-60 mph: 11.0 seconds
Top speed .... approx. 115 mph
Fuel mileage .... 12-16 mpg

★★★   **1959 Electra 225**
convertible
★★   **Electra Riviera hardtop**

Chapter 14

1959-60 Electra

History

The old General Motors compared favorably in many ways with the GM of today. One example is the old GM's understanding that although body sharing was inevitable, each division nevertheless must retain its own distinct look. Thus, the 1959 Buicks were distinct unto themselves—even though the 1959 Fisher A-, B-, and C-bodies were used up and down the GM line.

Ed Ragsdale had made the decision to scrap the traditional Buick model names for

This immaculate 1959 Electra 225 convertible is owned by Palmer Carlson. In this year, Buick broke further with the past, forsaking traditional model names and switching from the conventional crossbraced frame to a perimeter frame. Coil spring suspension remained, though some 225s had troublesome air bellows rear suspension. *Bud Juneau*

1959. In the nomenclature hierarchy, LeSabre replaced Special, Invicta replaced Century (and retained the senior Buick engine in a junior chassis), Electra replaced Super and Electra 225 (its length in inches) more or less replaced Roadmaster.

Ragsdale's successor, Ed Rollert, made strong efforts to upgrade quality and the state of Buick engineering. Styling, done by a team still led by the effective Ned Nickles, owed nothing to 1958 save the multi-chrome-block grille. From canted quad headlamps, the 1959 body swept smoothly back to end in a thin, concave tailfin. (All GM cars had fins in 1959, but none of the other fins matched Buick's for clean style.) New, too, was the Wildcat 401 V-8, Buick's first 400-plus engine, a bored and stroked 364 offering 325 hp, 445 lb-ft of torque and improved smoothness.

Although the 1960 facelift saw the 225 somewhat gaudier and less "pure," the car remained a stunning improvement on late-fifties Buicks. Production bounded up in 1959, checked slightly in 1960 and zoomed skyward in successive years.

Identification

The 225 was the only Electra convertible. In 1959, Electra 225 appeared in chrome on

Only 50 chrome squares can be counted on the 1959 nose, down from the 1958 count. After you get over this front end, the Electra is a smoothly styled car—probably the best effort by General Motors in that infamous year when tailfins soared. *Bud Juneau*

the lower front fender molding. In 1960, a massive chrome plate ran from the front to the rear fender and ventiports returned (four stylized decorative ones on the front fenders). Two four-door styles were offered: standard (broadly wrapped backlight

Let's put up the top. . . . Massive doors swing wide to let you into the leather-swathed interior. No expense was spared to make this top-line 1959 purely luxurious. The convertible's base price was $4,200, which is $15,000 in today's money—and that $15,000 would just about buy you one like this in 1988. . . .

. . . There. The 225 is one of the few ragtops that look as good with the top up or down. Value-wise, this car is a genuine sleeper. With Cadillacs of the same vintage going for up to $50,000, this handsome convertible, which is far better looking, ought to move up strongly in price over the next decade. *Bud Juneau*

and thin, probably structurally weak, C-pillars) and Riviera (conventional roofline with small triangular rear quarter-lights). New for 1960 was the adjustable Mirro-magic instrument panel, which could be adjusted to the easiest reading position with a turn-switch.

Performance and utility

A semi-perimeter-type frame replaced the previous straight girder crossbraced frame

in 1959 to provide a lower floor and a commensurately lower car; however, retention of torque tube drive and all-coil suspension gave ride and handling characteristics similar to those of previous Buicks. The air suspension option was dropped, but some 225s had the compromise self-leveling air bellows rear suspension, which was deleted from the 1960 option list. The 1960 models had independent front and rear heater controls and five air conditioner outlets, of which three were directionally adjustable, providing unprecedented climate control. Revised Saginaw power steering made for lower steering effort but also less road feel.

Problem areas

Many collectors say these are "darn good Buicks." The heating, ventilating and air-conditioning system is first-rate; however, the air bellows rear suspension is a noted source of problems, when so-equipped—avoid it if you can. Highly complicated electrics will be a nightmare if they act up; check every switch and servo carefully before you buy, and adjust your offer accordingly. Check all the usual places for rust, because

Hallmarks of the 1959 are shown here. The stylized knight's-helmet badge for the rear appears to have been partly inspired by the Mercedes tri-star, and the turbo-like wheel covers had small pot metal spinners affixed to their centers. These items are fairly easy to replace. *Bud Juneau*

Compared with clumsy workouts on other 1959 GM cars, the Buick tail was admirably styled— if a bit heavy on the chromium. Taillights were Ford-like but suited the projectile rear fender shape. The deck lid was broad and the cargo compartment was rather flat. *Bud Juneau*

An optional tissue dispenser swings out from underneath the dash at the center. Electric window lift controls are grouped on the driver's door armrest. *Bud Juneau*

Buick stayed with needle gauges in 1959, but the speedometer was the hard-to-read thermometer type. The small circular housings flanking the gauges contain a light knob (left) and a clock (right). *Bud Juneau*

these cars are prone to it. (See also engine notes under Problem areas in Chapter 12.)

Summary and prospects

Hobby price guides tend to overstate the value of most Buicks from this period and,

curiously, place the 1960 Electra 225 convertible about fifteen percent higher than the 1959 model. This may mean that the smoothly styled 1959 is a bargain compared with the confusing facelift of 1960 model,

The best angle for the 1959 is the rear three-quarter. Tailfins were huge, but were smoothly integrated into the body and were much better

done than those of the Cadillac and the 1959 Chrysler products. This is a car to watch in the years ahead. *Bud Juneau*

The Electra convertible for 1960 harked back to earlier themes by reviving portholes—sort of; these were actually simple brightmetal baubles mounted on the front fenders. Tailfins were toned down somewhat, the grille was simplified and quad lights were now horizontal rather than canted. Most hobby price guides place the 1960 ahead of the 1959 in value; I say the opposite.

but it is more likely that the price guides are inaccurate.

The 1959 had a somewhat lower production run and is regarded by many as one of the best looking Buicks. It is one to look for. The convertible will surely appreciate at a healthy clip in the nineties. The Riviera-type sedan is preferable, from a structural standpoint, to the glassback standard sedan, although the latter is more "period" in style.

1959-60 Electra 225 convertible

Engine
Type ..... eight-cylinder V-type, water-cooled, cast-iron block and heads
Bore and stroke .... 4.19x3.64 in.
Displacement .... 401.0 ci
Valve operation .... overhead
Compression ratio 10.5:1 (1959), 10.25:1 (1960)
Carburetion .... 4-bbl downdraft
Brake horsepower .... 325 gross @ 4400 rpm
Chassis and drivetrain
Transmission .... Dynaflow
Rear axle ratio .... 3.23:1, 2.78:1 (opt. 1959 Triple Turbine Dynaflow)
Front suspension .... independent, coil springs, tube shocks
Rear suspension ..... live axle, coil springs, tube shocks
Dimensions and weight
Wheelbase .... 126.3 in.
Overall length .... 225.4-225.9 in.
Track .... 62 in. front, 60 in. rear
Tire size 8.00x15
Curb weight .... 4562-4571 lb.
Performance
Acceleration .... 0-60 mph: 12.0 seconds
Top speed .... approx. 118 mph
Fuel mileage .... 14-19 mpg

Production

	1959	1960
Electra 225 convertible	5,493	6,746
Riviera four-door hardtop	6,324	8,029
Standard four-door hardtop	10,491	5,841

Chapter 15

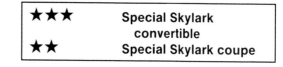

| ★★★ | Special Skylark convertible |
| ★★ | Special Skylark coupe |

1961-63 Special Skylark

History

Just a little bit longer, wider, faster and more luxurious than the plebian Corvair, the 1961 Special was a distinctly Buick answer to the newly born demand for compact cars. This car was not compact in the world sense, but with a 112 inch wheelbase it was one of the smallest Big Three models since before World War II.

The top-of-the-line Special was the handsome Skylark, Buick's offering to that large chunk of the marketplace craving bucket seats and custom trim plus power—in this case the spunky aluminum V-8. The formula

This chiseled side profile of the 1961 Skylark shows the car's Buick heritage (portholes, sort of), and its close design relationship to the larger Buicks that year. Luxurious bucket-seated interior, carpets and full vinyl upholstery were part of this attractive, highly salable package. Collectors still like them.

worked. In 1962 the Skylark coupe was the best-selling Special.

Offered beginning in March 1961 as a pillared coupe, the Skylark was distinctive with its "floating" horizontal-bar grille (standardized across the board on 1962 Specials), a padded vinyl top and bucket seats. A convertible body style and an optional four-speed manual gearbox were added for 1962, but the Skylark did not offer Buick's new V-6 as an option, retaining its aluminum V-8. Styling of the 1963 version was more conventional, but rather slab-sided and uninteresting. Although the Special was the most popular of the Buick-Olds-Pontiac compacts, a fickle market dictated that GM turn back to larger sizes, and the restyled 1964s were intermediates rather than compacts.

Identification

For 1961, the Special Skylark used a standard vinyl top on a pillared coupe body, a floating grille and Skylark badges. For the

Instant identification of the 1961 Skylark is provided by the wraparound brightmetal extensions of the taillamps, not present on the ordi-nary Special. Also unique was the vinyl top, which carried a Skylark badge on the rear roof quarters.

1962-63 convertible and pillarless hardtops, Skylark badges were used. Wraparound taillights appeared on the 1962 model, occasional bench seats on 1963s. All three years carried traditional triple ventiports on the front fenders.

Performance and utility

Arch Brown, writing in *Special Interest Autos*, June 1985, pointed out that the Skylark's light body and drivetrain gave it only fifteen pounds per horsepower, against over twenty on the Chevy Impala, America's standard at that time. This translated into brisk performance, with *Road & Track* recording 0-60 mph in 10.2 seconds and a top speed of 107 mph with the 1962 four-speed (although the editors thought that little performance was sacrificed when the Skylark was equipped with Buick's excellent Dual Path Turbine Drive three-speed automatic transmission, notably smooth and reliable).

Reasonably sized by today's standards, the Skylark returned excellent fuel economy and offered smooth, comfortable accommodation for five. It was also a remarkably quiet car, even by today's standards.

Problem areas

Skylark-only body hardware is the biggest problem faced by an owner trying to put one of these in shape. The stuff was not of good quality, and few new-old-stock replacements exist.

The aluminum V-8 was basically a good engine—witness its longevity from the Skylark to the current English Range Rover. But it did have corrosion and reliability problems, and incompletely cleaned blocks at the foundry could cause real trouble by leaving machining chips inside the castings after assembly. When these chips inevitably got into the radiator, they would react electrolytically with the copper core, causing block-

Virtually no change at all occurred on the Skylark in 1962, but narrow-band whitewalls arrived, and collectors should equip their 1962 with these for strict accuracy. The convertible leads in value as you would expect, being about twice as costly today as the coupe in equivalent condition.

age and cooling problems. This could happen over a long period of time, and may just be starting in long-stored low-mileage examples. Pay close attention to the cooling system and be sure the radiator is flushed and clean. To retard corrosion, use 100 percent antifreeze for the coolant.

Summary and prospects

Quirky but individual 1961-62 styling is strongly preferred to the more ordinary 1963 variety. This means that the 1962 convertible is the most desirable Skylark, especially when fitted with the optional four-speed manual gearbox. Such models in fine original condition can cost $10,000 today.

The 1963 was more conventional inside, too—you had to pay extra for bucket seats, for example—but the fine original example should not be passed over in favor of a rough 1962. At about $7,500 for the best one in the world, the 1963 Skylark convertible is a bargain among Buick collector cars; less perfect but worthwhile examples can be found for as little as $3,000.

Both years have slow but steady prospects for value appreciation in the immediate future.

Production

	1961	1962	1963
Special Skylark convertible	—	8,913	10,212
1962-63 Special Skylark coupe hardtop	12,683	34,060	32,109

1961-63 Special Skylark

Engine
Type .... eight-cylinder V-type, water-cooled, aluminum block and heads
Bore and stroke .... 3.50x2.80 in.
Displacement .... 215.0 ci
Valve operation .... overhead
Compression ratio 10.25:1 (1961), 11:1 (1961-63)
Carburetion .... 4-bbl downdraft
Brake horsepower .... 185 gross @ 4800 rpm (1961), 190 gross @ 4800 rpm (1961), 200 gross @ 5000 rpm (1962)
Chassis and drivetrain
Transmission .... three-speed std.; Dynaflow opt.; four-speed opt. (1962-63)
Rear axle ratio .... 3.36:1 (man.), 3.08:1 (auto.)

Chassis and drivetrain
Front suspension .... independent, coil springs, tube shocks
Rear suspension ..... live axle, coil springs, tube shocks
Dimensions and weight
Wheelbase .... 112.1 in.
Overall length ...... 188.4 in. (1961-62), 192.1 in. (1963)
Track .... 56 in. front, 56 in. rear
Tire size 6.50x13
Curb weight .... 2687-2871 lb.
Performance
Acceleration .... 0-60 mph: 10 seconds (man.), 11-12 seconds (auto.)
Top speed .... approx. 105 mph
Fuel mileage .... 16-20 mpg

★★	1962 Special
	convertible
★	1963 Special
	convertible

1962-63 Special convertible

History

From some perspectives, a unit-body/chassis convertible is a contradiction in terms, but the Special's method of construction was such that the softtop version, which appeared in its second year of production, was particularly tight and quiet—characteristics not typical of convertibles. This model was offered in both standard and deluxe trim stages, easily told apart by the chrome molding halfway up the body sides of the deluxe.

The aluminum V-8 was available in two states of tune. This was also the first Special model with the new V-6 engine, an important engine in Buick history, a fine combination of economy and performance and the first V-6 in a volume American car. (The V-6's tooling was later sold to American Motors, but was dramatically reacquired by Buick during the 1973 energy crisis and reinstalled in the original machinery locating holes on the floor of Buick's Flint factory.)

The 1961 Special was outsold by all rival compacts save the low-volume Dodge Lancer, F-85 and Studebaker Lark. In 1962, however, it surpassed the Valiant in sales—which was going some—owing its success in part to the fine new V-6 as well as sporty models like this convertible.

Identification

Special script appeared on the front fenders. No brightmetal taillight trim wrapped around the rear fenders as on Skylarks. The 1963 version (sold in standard form only) may be quickly distinguished from the Skylark convertible by its lack of bodyside brightmetal molding. (See also notes on 1962-63 Specials in the Identification section of Chapter 15.)

Performance and utility

This model was the first Special to carry the new V-6 when it appeared in mid-model-year, but that engine at first came only with the three-speed manual shifter. The optional V-8 could be had with automatic and four-speed as well as three-speed. Performance was excellent with the V-8, sprightly with the V-6.

Like the Skylark, the Special convertible offered pleasant top-down travel for five, with excellent performance and remarkable silence and smoothness as compared with rival compacts.

Problem areas

See Problem areas in Chapter 15.

Summary and prospects

Lawrence Gustin of Buick Public Relations, co-author of *The Buick*, suggested the

Buick's pretty 1962 Special convertible is lost in the relative popularity of the 1962 Skylark, but it's almost equally desirable, to many better looking and costs less (you can plan on paying 20 to 25 percent less than for a comparable 1962 Skylark, 10 to 15 percent less than for a 1963 Skylark). Both convertibles arrived in the second year of the Special, 1962. A major face-lift made both look relatively ordinary in 1963, so 1962s outpace 1963s in value by about 50 percent. The top price for a near-perfect 1962 Special convertible was $10,000 in 1988, but you should be able to bargain or shop for less. The 1963 will cost much less—and rightfully so, since it's far less distinctive.

inclusion of the Special convertible, remembering that it was his first new car. "It was extremely attractive," he wrote. "In fact I think it looks better than the Skylark which had some wraparound chrome near the taillights that I found unattractive. But its styling was unfortunately gone by '63 and completely changed by '64." With this in mind, I rate the 1962 Special convertible twice as high as the 1963.

The good news is that the Special is still a sleeper, outshone in the collector market by the desirable Skylark, and is therefore quite a buy. While a super nice 1962 Skylark convertible may sell for five figures, a 1962 Special convertible in the same condition will be $1,000 to $2,000 less, perhaps $3,000 less if it's the standard trim version. The 1963 model came only in standard trim, and the value spread between it and the 1963 Skylark convertible is smaller: $6,000 for a nice Special, say, against about $7,500 for a Skylark. The gap between Skylark and Special convertibles will widen over the next decade, so the Special convertible will remain a good value for the money, if not an investment-quality model.

Production

	1962	1963
Special standard trim	7,918	8,082
Special deluxe trim	8,332	—

1962-63 Special convertible

Engine

Type . . . . . . six-cylinder V-type, water-cooled, cast-iron block and heads std.; V-8 opt. (see specifications for 1961-63 Special Skylark)
Bore and stroke . . . . 3.63x3.20 in.
Displacement . . . . 198.0 ci
Valve operation . . . . overhead
Compression ratio 8.8:1
Carburetion . . . . 2-bbl downdraft
Brake horsepower . . . . 135 gross @ 4600 rpm

Chassis and drivetrain

Transmission . . . . three-speed std. with V-6; auto. and four-speed opt. with V-8
Rear axle ratio . . . . 3.36:1 (man. 1962), 3.23:1 (man. 1963), 3.08:1 (auto.)

Chassis and drivetrain

Front suspension . . . . independent, coil springs, tube shocks
Rear suspension . . . . . live axle, coil springs, tube shocks

Dimensions and weight

Wheelbase . . . . 112.1 in.
Overall length . . . . 188.4 in. (1962), 192.1 in. (1963)
Track . . . . 56 in. front, 56 in. rear
Tire size 6.50x13
Curb weight . . . . 2768-2858 lb.

Performance

Acceleration . . . . 0-60 mph: 13-15 seconds (V-6), 10-12 seconds (V-8)
Top speed . . . . approx. 95 mph
Fuel mileage . . . . 20-22 mpg

Chapter 17

1962-64 Wildcat

History

An example of the bucket-seat-and-console formula applied to a full-size Buick, the Wildcat was a fast and furious powerhouse, a kind of "Century for the sixties," using the senior engine in the junior Buick body. Taking its name from the concurrent big-block, the Wildcat arrived as a trim variation of the Invicta hardtop in 1962. It was priced at close to $4,000 base, the most expensive Invicta in the line. Standard were bucket front seats, a vinyl top, special Wildcat indentification and the hot 325 hp 401 V-8.

The same pattern governed 1963, when the Wildcat was broken out as a separate range and a four-door hardtop and convertible were added. In 1964, the Invicta having vanished entirely, there was a Wildcat four-

The 1963 Wildcat four-door hardtop is shown here. The Wildcat appeared little different from the Invicta in 1962, but in 1963 it was distinguished by brushed aluminum fender and deck panels. The Wildcat and Invicta became a separate series in 1963, including two-door hardtop and convertible models as well as four-door hardtops. Only the convertibles have come close to five-figure values so far; a hardtop like this should run you less than $5,000, and good ones can be found for little more than half that much.

The potent 1963 Wildcat was a hot, full-size Buick conceived in the image of the Oldsmobile Starfire, Ford Galaxie 500 and "non-letter series" Chrysler 300. Luxurious bucket-seated interior was part of the package. Wildcats are still remarkably cheap on the collector market, but try to get one in excellent original condition.

door sedan. The following year, the series blossomed into a full range of rather less distinguished land yachts.

Since collectors like limited editions with high performance, I recommend the 1962-64 Wildcats. But this should not stop you from considering that extra-nice post-1964 model, especially if it's a convertible.

Identification

In 1962, these cars had Wildcat emblems on the roof quarters, special Wildcat wheel covers, an identifying front fender script, chromed headliner bows and a standard vinyl top. In 1963, they had all of the above plus a special grille with heavy horizontal bars and a Wildcat emblem. In 1964, they had the same plus ribbed, wide lower body molding and Wildcat emblems on the roof quarters (or on convertibles, on the lower front fenders).

Performance and utility

This model was very fast, but not impossible to stop thanks to oversize aluminum brakes (about the best drum brakes in the industry, although not quite up to the fade-resistance of discs). If not quite able to leap tall buildings at a single bound, the Wildcat was fairly capable of cruising at 100 mph—at

commensurate expense in fuel. It had limited passenger capacity owing to its interior console, but plenty of room for four people and all the luggage they could carry. Despite sporty pretensions, automatic transmission was standard.

Problem areas

The 401 V-8 tends to be longer-lived and more reliable than the 425, which was at its limits of block expansion. The 425's cylinder walls were relatively thin and its heads did not provide the airflow it needed. Cylinder volume had so outpaced valve size that engineers nicknamed the 425 the nailhead engine. The smallish valves caused Buick to resort to valve timing that contributed to rough low-rpm running. On the other hand, the 425's piston rings had better oil control and the engine was not as prone to burning oil as was the 401. Its very high compression means poor running with most modern fuels.

Quality control plagued Buick throughout this period, and interior fit and finish, even of fine original cars, may disconcert some owners.

Summary and prospects

This model was never a blue-chip collectible, but is well worth considering if you like

The 1964 Wildcats carried distinguishing triple moldings on the front fenders. Optional, but often fitted, were chrome-plated mag-type wheels. Wildcat badges were on the rear roof quarters. The 425 V-8 was an option in 1964, but the 401 (which had powered Wildcats since 1962) is recommended.

1962-64 Wildcat

Engine
Type ..... eight-cylinder V-type, water-cooled, cast-iron block and heads
Bore and stroke .... 4.19x3.64 in., 4.31x3.64 in. (opt. 1964)
Displacement .... 401.0 ci, 425.0 ci (opt. 1964)
Valve operation .... overhead
Compression ratio 10.25:1
Carburetion ..... 4-bbl downdraft; two 4-bbl (opt. 1964)
Brake horsepower .... 325 gross @ 4400 rpm, 360 gross @ 4600 rpm (opt. 1964)

Chassis and drivetrain
Transmission ..... auto. Turbine 300; Turbine 400 (opt.)
Rear axle ratio .... 2.78:1 std.
Front suspension .... independent, coil springs, tube shocks
Rear suspension ..... live axle, coil springs, tube shocks

Dimensions and weight
Wheelbase .... 123 in.
Overall length .... 214 in. (1962), 215.7 in. (1963), 218.8 in. (1964)
Track .... 62.1 in. front, 61 in. rear
Tire size 7.60x15
Curb weight .... 4003-4228 lb.

Performance
Acceleration .... 0-60 mph: 9-10 seconds
Top speed .... approx. 115-120 mph
Fuel mileage .... 10-17 mpg

your cars big with performance to match. Wildcat convertibles in the best possible condition have yet to go into five figures in the collector market, and decent ones can be had for $5,000 on up. Hardtops are readily available and cost as little as $2,500, since the market for Detroit boats bottomed in the late seventies and has never recovered, even among collectors.

Production

	1962	1963	1964
Convertible	—	6,021	7,850
Two-door hardtop	4,000	12,185	22,893
Four-door hardtop	—	17,519	33,358
Four-door sedan	—	—	20,144

Chapter 18

1963-65 Riviera

History

A watershed design for Buick and the industry, the Riviera revived the personal luxury theme, setting a sales pace that everyone else (including the Ford Thunderbird) had to follow. Ironically, its progenitor, project car XP-715, started life as a potential Cadillac, with GM design chief Bill Mitchell even considering calling it a LaSalle. Buick got it because Buick needed it (and because Cadillac refused it).

Buick engineers deserve full marks for creating in the Riviera a notable car of its era. As its basis they used a stiffened Electra chassis, shortened fourteen inches to only 208 inches—quite compact for a big Buick. The crisp styling was inspired by razor-edge designs like that of the Rolls-Bentley, translated into a uniquely GM look by the wizards —notably Ned Nickles—working for Bill Mitchell at the Warren, Michigan, Tech Center.

Powered by Buick's big engines, the Riviera offered smoking performance: 120 mph top speed, 100 mph cruising speed, 0-100 mph in twenty-five seconds, the standing

The original Riviera, the 1963, was the first complete ground-up design project from GM styling after Bill Mitchell took over, and it is a splendid testimony to Mitchell's ideas. Flawless from almost every angle, it had a conservative shape but one in which no detail was jarring or out of place.

quarter-mile in sixteen seconds at 85 mph. These were the most typical figures, although some road tests reported quarter-mile times as low as 15.2 seconds at 92 mph.

The R-in-an-oval motif was repeated in the wheel covers, whose turbo-blade design was unchanged from that in 1963. *Bud Juneau*

Zero-to-sixty took between 7.5 and 8.5 seconds, depending on the engine, the back axle and the weight of one's right foot, as well as one's degree of fearlessness with the standard automatic transmission. Fuel mileage averaged around 15 mpg, provided you didn't perform too many brave antics.

The most developed version was the 1965 Gran Sport, option package A9, which included the twin four-barrel-carb 360 hp V-8, a beefed-up Turbine Drive, large-diameter dual exhausts, Posi-traction, a 3.42:1 final drive ratio (3.58:1 optional), brightmetal engine accents, ribbed valve covers, Gran Sport badges and special wheel covers. Only 3,335 Gran Sports were built in 1965; today they are the most collectible of Rivieras.

Fast, comfortable and beautiful, the first-generation Riviera was among the first Milestone cars, and remains a sought-after postwar Buick.

Identification

In 1963, Riviera appeared in block letters on the deck lid. In 1964, a new R-in-oval

A beautiful 1964 Riviera owned by Palmer Carlson of Santa Rosa, California, painted the typical Riviera white, shows that few design changes occurred in the car's second year. One obvious change was a stand-up hood ornament with the Riviera R enclosed in an oval. Headlamps were still in the fixed position. *Bud Juneau*

Another identifying feature of the 1964 was the Riviera name in script on the right rear deck lid, which replaced the block letter name in the center of the 1963 deck lid. *Bud Juneau*

A profile view of Carlson's Riviera shows that the car's extreme cleanliness and integrity of line were unaltered in 1964. GM was breaking new styling ground here, daring to defy the American tradition of drastic model year change. To some extent the new philosophy may not have worked, since sales declined slightly in 1964 despite Flint's ability to build more Rivieras. *Bud Juneau*

The final 1965 version of the first-generation Riviera shows an obvious change: headlamps were stacked vertically and hidden behind the shells mounted outboard in the front fenders. The hood ornament was also changed, becoming smaller. *Bud Juneau*

badge appeared on the hood, taillights and wheel covers, and Riviera script replaced the block letters on the deck and was added to the front fenders. In 1965, hidden headlamps were featured, along with a new, massive rear bumper encompassing the headlamps. This rear-end treatment replaced the separate taillamps and slim nerf-type 1963-64 bumper. (Enthusiasts have their various loyalties, but many say the hidden headlamps gained more than the clumsy back end lost.)

Custom interior models (see Summary and prospects in this chapter) may be identified by two interior handles on each door.

Performance and utility

The 1963s used the old-style Turbine Drive two-speed automatic, a five-element torque converter, which produced somewhat better acceleration times than did the Twin Turbine Hydra-matic that replaced it in 1964. All Rivieras were fast, capable road cars with fine combinations of ride and handling, but because of its lower axle ratio, the Gran Sport ironically had a lower top speed than did the standard car.

Buick did not equip the Gran Sport with anything special in the way of suspension, although a handling package (stiffer springs and shocks, a thicker front antiroll bar) was optional, and a 15:1 steering ratio was available to improve on the somewhat numb standard Saginaw power unit.

Problem areas

The 1964-65 Twin Turbine Hydra-matic was smoother and less prone to trouble than was the 1963 Turbine Drive, and it was especially rugged in its beefed-up form on the 1965 Gran Sport. (See also engine notes under Problem areas in Chapter 17.) Rivieras are moderately prone to rust, and the potential purchaser should look for it. Another source of incidental trouble is the complicated electrical system.

This was a relatively complex car, expensive to restore. The low-mileage original example is a better buy at twice the price of the well-worn model.

Summary and prospects

Had Buick built a convertible, fine copies would today be selling for well into five figures. As hardtops, however, the best Rivieras presently top out around $7,000. One hobby price guide pegs a 1965 Gran Sport in ninety-point condition at $7,500, but that really is the limit.

In constant dollars, therefore, a top-condition Riviera is now selling for about forty percent of its value when new, which means it's one of the best buys around among high-potential postwar collector cars. Sooner or later the market is going to realize this—so the faster you find yours, the better! Look for rapid appreciation in the next decade, especially among Gran Sports.

Certain low-volume Riviera options are worth seeking out, including the custom interior. This option package included leather upholstery in 1963 and fancy cloth or vinyl in 1964-65, along with oiled walnut veneer trim in all three years. The 1965 custom interior came with a broad ribbed rocker panel molding, but this is not itself evidence of the custom interior since it was available individually. A sure way of identifying the package is to count the interior door handles: all custom interiors had two on each door, one at each end of the long armrest. Other worthwhile Riviera options are the wooden steering wheel, rear window defroster, rear speaker with reverberator, wire wheel covers and, in 1965, chromed steel road wheels.

As Churchill said, it is much better making predictions afterward rather than ahead of time. Nevertheless, here is one I don't mind chancing: by the year 2000, ninety-five-point original Riviera Gran Sports are going to be selling for over $50,000, which is about double what a $7,500 certificate of deposit at eight percent interest will have earned by then—and you can't drive a CD!

Production

	1963	1964	1965
Riviera two-door hardtop	40,000	37,658	34,586*

Includes 3,335 Gran Sports and 3,808 non-Gran Sports with 360 hp engines

---

1963-65 Riviera

Engine
Type ..... eight-cylinder V-type, water-cooled, cast-iron block and heads
Bore and stroke .... 4.19x3.64 in. (1963, 1965), 4.31x3.64 in. (1963-64, 1965 Gran Sport)
Displacement ...... 401 ci (1963, 1965), 425 ci (1963-64, 1965 Gran Sport)
Valve operation .... overhead
Compression ratio 10.25:1
Carburetion .... 4-bbl; two 4-bbl (opt. 1965)
Brake horsepower ... 325 gross @ 4400 rpm (1963, 1965), 340 gross @ 4400 rpm (1964), 360 gross @ 4600 rpm (1965)

Chassis and drivetrain
Transmission .... Turbine Drive (1963), Twin Turbine (1964-65)
Rear axle ratio .... 3.23:1 (1963), 3.08:1, 3.42:1 (Gran Sport), 3.58:1 opt. (Gran Sport)
Front suspension .... independent, coil springs, tube shocks and anti-sway bar
Rear suspension .... live axle, coil springs, tube shocks, radius arms and one upper torque arm

Dimensions and weight
Wheelbase .... 117 in.
Overall length .... 208-209 in.
Track .... 60 in. front, 59 in. rear
Tire size 7.10x15 (1963-64), 8.45x15 (1965)
Curb weight .... 3951-4036 lb.

Performance
Acceleration .... 0-60 mph: 7.0-8.8 seconds
Top speed .... approx. 120 mph
Fuel mileage .... 12-16 mpg

★★★★	**GS400 convertible**
★★★	**Gran Sport, GS340**
	convertible
★★	**Skylark Gran Sport**
	hardtops, coupes

1965-67 Skylark Gran Sport

History

The Gran Sport was a shot in the arm for Buick's lagging compact—at least in the opinion of collectors, who tend to view the post-1963 Specials as duller than dishwater (which by and large they were). The Gran Sport began as a modest $200.53 option package for the sportier Skylarks, ending up as a super-muscle-car, what *Car Life* called "Buick's hope of the 1967 model year." The heart of the package was most often a 400 ci V-8. Initially, your money also bought a three-speed all-synchromesh transmission, a beefed-up chassis and rear axle, revised springs and shock absorbers, oversize tires on six-inch-wide rims and special exterior trimwork.

In terms of sales, the Skylark Gran Sport started strong, racking up more than 70,000 customers in its introductory year, but the muscle car market peaked almost as soon as it got started. In 1966, sales plunged to fewer

The 1965 Skylark Gran Sport sported red-filled script on deck and coupe roof quarters (moved to rear fenders on convertibles). Taillights were wall-to-wall. This hardtop represents the most popular of all Gran Sports; it achieved almost 50,000 sales, nearly five times the figure of any other Gran Sport. The year 1965 was simultaneously the first and best year for muscle cars, whose sales tailed off rapidly through the rest of the decade. Good news is that nice 1965 hardtops like this can still be bought for the price of a current Buick's down payment.

than 14,000, creating some rarities (see Production in this chapter), and although Buick tried to expand the formula with a junior-version GS340 in 1967, nothing much resulted. In later years the package was spun off as a separate Gran Sport series (see Chapter 20), but volume never approached that of banner year 1965. There are probably more customers for the Gran Sport today than there were twenty years ago.

Identification

In 1965, special red Gran Sport emblems appeared on the dash, grille, deck and roof quarters (coupes) or rear fenders (convertibles). In 1966, emblems were used on the rear quarter panels and dash plus the matte-black rear cover panel, and bucket seats were optional. In 1967, the GS340 had full rear wheel cutouts, Rally stripes and hood scoops, plus special badging and Rally-style wheels. The 1967 GS400 was similar, with the addition of Wide Oval redline or white-line tires on Rally wheels.

Performance and utility

General Manager Ed Rollert called it "a completely engineered performance car," but for the Skylark, performance meant mere acceleration—not handling, braking or high-speed stability. At about 12.5 pounds per horsepower, the car couldn't help but be fast off the line. Like most muscle cars it was unrefined, however, and today's collector should recognize its limitations as well as its merits. As to its positive side, what about 0-60 mph in six seconds and a 100 mph, 14.7 second standing quarter-mile?

Disc brakes were optional on 1967 models and are definitely worth looking for on your potential purchase. Expect a hard ride and no real comfort, and plan to prefer laying rubber on the strip to cruising mountain highways at 100 plus.

Problem areas

Buick intermediates of this period are mechanically reliable but susceptible to rust, and the potential purchase needs to be examined carefully, unless it is from California, the Southwest or that island of dryness in central Georgia and Florida. Check calipers of disc-brake-equipped cars for corrosion and wear, and rotors for deformity. Check brakes and engines with the view that most Gran Sports tend to have been run hard earlier in their lives. Interiors make wide use of vinyl and hold up well. Almost all body hardware is impossible to find as new-old-stock, though sheet metal parts are available.

Summary and prospects

A mid-level investment among the muscle cars, packing more appreciation potential

The Skylark Gran Sport for 1966 got a heavy facelift receiving a longer body despite retention of the 115 inch wheelbase. The roofline was now more swoopy than angular, but had somehow lost the 1965's distinction.

than some big-engined intermediates but less than neoclassics like the Pontiac GTO and Oldsmobile 4-4-2, the Gran Sport is a good bet if you can't afford the prices GTOs and 4-4-2s now command. Gran Sport prices are about $5,000 for a ninety-five percent perfect coupe and about $7,000 for a convertible. These are roughly $3,000 less, car for car, than the prices of comparable GTOs.

Gran Sports are probably destined to appreciate at a rate double that of inflation, so they are sound investments while also providing greasy-kid entertainment and stump-pulling acceleration.

Production

	1965	1966	1967
Gran Sport and 1967 GS400 convertible	10,456	2,047	2,140
Gran Sport and 1967 GS400 coupe	11,877	1,835	1,014
Gran Sport and 1967 GS400 hardtop	47,034	9,934	10,659
1967 GS340 hardtop	—	—	3,692

1966-67 Skylark Gran Sport

Engine

Type . . . . . eight-cylinder V-type, water-cooled, cast-iron block and heads
Bore and stroke . . . . 4.19x3.64 in. (1965-66), 3.75x3.85 in. (1967 GS340), 4.04x3.90 in. (1967 GS400)
Displacement . . . . 400 ci (1965-66), 340 ci (1967 GS340), 399.7 ci (1967 GS400)
Valve operation . . . . overhead
Compression ratio 10.25:1
Carburetion 4-bbl
Brake horsepower . . . . . 325 gross @ 4400 rpm (1965-66), 260 gross @ 4200 rpm (1967 GS340), 340 gross @ 5000 rpm (1967 GS400)

Chassis and drivetrain

Transmission . . . . three-speed man. (std.); Turbine auto. (opt. 1966-67); four-speed man. (opt. 1966, 1967 GS400 only)
Rear axle ratio . . . . 3.08:1 (1965-66), 3.36:1 opt. (1965-66), 3.23:1 (1967 GS340), 3.36:1 opt. (1967 GS340), 3.90:1 opt. (1967 GS340), 3.36:1 std. man. (1967 GS400), 2.93:1 std.

Chassis and drivetrain

(1967 GS400), 3.36:1 opt. auto. (1967 GS400), 3.55 opt. on all (1967 GS400), 3.90 opt. on all (1967 GS400), 4.30 opt. on all (1967 GS400)
Front suspension . . . . independent, coil springs, tube shocks and anti-sway bar
Rear suspension . . . . four-link live axle, coil springs, tube shocks

Dimensions and weight

Wheelbase . . . . 115 in.
Overall length . . . . 203.5 in. (1965-66), 205 in. (1967)
Track . . . . . . 58 in. front, 58 in. rear (1965-66); 58 in. front, 59 in. rear (1967)
Tire size 7.75x14 (1965-67), F70x14 (1967 GS400)
Curb weight . . . 3720 lb. (1965-67), 3765 lb. (1967 GS400)

Performance

Acceleration . . . . 0-60 mph: 7.8 seconds (1965-67), 6.0 seconds (1967 GS400)
Top speed . . . . approx. 110-115 mph
Fuel mileage . . . . 10-14 mpg

Physically almost the same for 1967, the Gran Sport now branched into the GS340 and GS400 (shown). The GS400 was offered as a coupe and convertible as well as a hardtop; the GS340 only as a hardtop. The new 400 block measured 4.04x3.90 and delivered 340 bhp, which was the highest yet. The GS400 hardtop sold 10,659 units, but sales of other 400s and the GS340 were minimal.

1966-67 Riviera

History

Rarely has one classic Detroit design immediately followed another—but this is one that did. The second-generation Riviera was, if anything, even purer and more elegant than the first. Its engineering benefited from all Buick had learned since 1963. Riviera fan Chris Wolfe writes that it looked "like a Motorama show car, not a production Buick." *Car Life* summarized its new

Sensational from stem to stern, the glamorous second-generation Riviera was a marvelous piece of redesign, and I think it's one of the most underrated (and undervalued) cars of the sixties. This one carries the all-vinyl interior.

Semi-fastback roof and rear deck, and the longest hood ever, characterized the new look for 1966. Every piece on the car was new, including the neatly integrated taillamps and the elegant wheel covers. Second-generation Rivieras carried no ventwings, flow-through ventilation having become standard.

sleekness as follows: "Where before it had a rather chamfered crispness to its tailored looks, it now is frankly sensuous in its sweeping lines." Designwise, it was as perfect as a car could be, the best single Detroit design in the sixties.

A Gran Sport option remained available, but it did not involve higher horsepower.

Detroit hardly ever answers one classic series with another just as good, but Buick did so with the second-generation Riviera for 1966. The 1967 model was not much altered. Headlamps went horizontal again, but were still hidden—outboard on the thin-bar grille, where their covering lids can just be seen in this photograph.

The 340 hp 425 was standard, except for a reported 198 cars fitted with twin Carter four-barrel carbs as a dealer-installed option (360 hp). That option was dropped in 1967 when Riviera received a new 430 V-8 with 360 hp standard. Gran Sport Rivieras for 1966 had a 3.42:1 final drive ratio, stiff springs and shocks, extra-large exhaust pipes, Goodyear Redline tires and Gran Sport identification. The almost-identical-looking 1967 Gran Sports offered similar equipment, with the options of a 3.91:1 final drive ratio and radial-ply tires. Flow-through ventilation eliminated ventwings on both models.

What splendid cars these were—and are! Today, their great contemporaries (the Coke-bottle-shaped Avanti, the Corvette Sting Ray, the Mustang) begin to look dated, while the Riviera remains fresh. One has to wonder why, after 1967, Buick insisted on changing anything.

Identification

The Riviera name is spelled in block letters on the 1966 hood, but offset in script on the 1967. The 1967 grille had bolder horizontal bars but deleted the horizontal-lined parking light lenses.

Performance and utility

I once owned a 1967 Riviera, all too briefly, having to part with it because as a daily driver its fuel thirst was prodigious (in those halcyon days it cost $7.50 to fill the tank!). I wish I still owned it, as a straight collector car. True, it was bigger and more of a handful than the 1963-65 models; nevertheless, it was great fun to drive and magnificent to look upon.

Performance was essentially the same as with the 1965 Gran Sport: 0-60 mph took eight seconds flat, the quarter-mile about sixteen seconds. It was strictly a four-passenger car, but those four traveled in the lap of luxury. One disconcerting feature was the huge door width, the largest in the industry at the time, always able to clip some other car in a parking lot or create a hazard for the driver who tried to exit after parking on a busy street.

Factory photograph of the 1966 Riviera Gran Sport, with optional wire wheel covers and what appears to be a full-vinyl interior. The GS badge looks as if it were airbrushed-in, but this is the correct style and position. Add 15 percent, car for car, to a Riviera's value if it carries Gran Sport equipment.

The Riviera in this period continued to offer a variety of interiors, although leather was not available. Full vinyl was standard, and cloth-and-vinyl made up the custom interior. There were also four varieties of front seat: buckets, bench, buckets with headrests and buckets with a reclining passenger seat. (The last three are quite scarce, but only the headrest option is hotly desired by collectors.)

Problem areas

The 1967's optional climate-control system was changed in mid-model-year, and was described only in a supplemental service manual that is scarce. Both the original and the modified system required special diagnostic equipment and parts, then available only at Buick shops and today virtually non-existent. A minor problem with the 430 engine was oil starvation at the rocker arm bases, but by and large both big-blocks were sturdy, long-lived units. Electrical faults bedevil a number of cars (on my 1967, the electric window lifts failed regularly in the wet).

This generation Riviera is a ruster, but not so much so as the 1963-65 series. The body should be thoroughly gone over, as always, especially if the car spent its life in the Northeast.

Summary and prospects

If the 1963-65 Riviera is a bargain, the 1966-67 Riviera is the steal of the century. The highest price quoted by any hobby source for the best-possible-condition Gran Sport was $6,300, and non-Gran Sport models are pegged around $4,000 to $5,000. Some Gran Sports have been offered in places like *Hemmings Motor News* for $6,000 or so.

I can't believe people have so overlooked a car that is on every expert's list of great postwar designs. Here, then, is the second of only two predictions you will find in this book: By the year 2000, mint original 1966-67 Riviera Gran Sports will be hitting $50,000. Get one quick before the rest of those Buick collectors realize it!

Production

	1966	1967
Riviera two-door hard-top, 340 hp	45,150	—
Riviera two-door hard-top, 360 hp	198	42,799

1966-67 Riviera

Engine
Type ..... eight-cylinder V-type, water-cooled, cast-iron block and heads
Bore and stroke .... 4.31x3.64 in. (1966), 4.19x3.90 in. (1967)
Displacement .... 425 ci (1966), 430 ci (1967)
Valve operation .... overhead
Compression ratio 10.25:1 (1966), 10.5:1 (1967)
Carburetion .... 4-bbl; two 4-bbl opt. (1966)
Brake horsepower .... 340 gross @ 4400 rpm (1966), 360 gross @ 4600 rpm (1967, opt. 1966)
Chassis and drivetrain
Transmission .... Turbine auto.
Rear axle ratio .... 3.23:1, 3.42:1 (Gran Sport), 3.58:1 (opt. 1966), 3.91:1 (opt. 1967)
Front suspension .... independent, coil springs, tube shocks
Rear suspension .... four-link live axle, coil springs, tube shocks
Dimensions and weight
Wheelbase .... 119 in.
Overall length .... 211.1 in.
Track .... 63.5 in. front, 63 in. rear
Tire size and type .... 8.45x15 (600Lx15), 225Rx15 radials (opt. 1967)
Curb weight .... 4300 lb. (1966), 4230 lb. (1967)
Performance
Acceleration .... 0-60 mph: 8.5-9.5 seconds
Top speed .... approx. 120 mph
Fuel mileage .... 10-13 mpg

| ★★★ | **Gran Sport convertible** |
| ★★ | **Gran Sport coupe** |

1968-72 Gran Sport

History

In 1968-72, the Gran Sport muscle car was continued and broken out as a separate series using the new GM B-body with the 112 inch wheelbase for two-door models. The GS350 and GS400 offered a choice of Buick big-blocks in a sporty package, either a hardtop or a convertible (available as a

It is easy to identify the 1968 GS400: Look for special badges and a scoop just behind the front wheels. This new body style for Buick intermediates as a whole bowed to tradition by employing a sweepspearlike bodyside molding with useful effect. Over 90 percent of Gran Sport production was hardtops, and prices for these are presently flat. Convertibles will be hitting five figures shortly, however.

The 1969 GS350 had special badges moved to the rear fenders. Instant identification is possible by looking for the bold but clumsy egg-crate grillework, which was just as quickly drop-ped. Overall Gran Sport production barely broke 10,000 units in 1969, and production of the convertible (offered as a GS400 only) totaled a mere 1,776 units.

GS400 only). The usual identifying grille, scoops, stripes and badgework adorned the bodies, while potent engines gave hot off-the-line performance.

The bigger-engine model became the GS455 in 1970, when the 455 V-8 (the largest Flint engine to date) replaced the 430. It was the only Buick intermediate with that engine.

The line was rationalized to two models, a coupe and a convertible, in 1971. Both were called simply Gran Sports, but the 455 was available as an option. Sales were hardly worth recording (902 convertibles!).

Here is the 1970 GS455 hardtop. The basic 1967-68 body shell was retained for 1969 but was cleaned up with a fine mesh grille and a red-stripe rocker panel. Under the GS badge on the front fender is a small plaque reading "Stage 1." Stage 1 was Buick's option package for the big V-8, which included a special camshaft, a positive traction rear axle, a high-speed valvetrain and dual exhausts. Exactly 8,732 GS455 hardtops were built, along with 1,416 convertibles and 9,948 GS350 hardtops.

Small auxiliary grilles show up within the bumper on the 1971 Gran Sport. Note GS455 badging still on the fenders, although Buick didn't officially use the numbers in 1971. For the record, this car was, as it says on the grille, a "GS by Buick."

For 1972, the Gran Sport was merged back into the base compact line, known then as Skylark rather than Special. This was the end of the line, for muscle cars were by then almost unsalable. In 1973, the Skylark gave way to the Century intermediate, aimed at an older, more luxury-loving buyer.

Identification

In 1968, the GS350 badge was on the center of the deck lid, the GS400 badge was on the front fenders. In 1969, badges appeared as in 1968 and GS monograms were used on the grille and rear fenders. In 1970, matte-black grillework was used with GS initials on the left-hand side, and hood scoops and GS badges appeared. In 1971, appearance was similar to that in 1970 with red-filled brightmetal rocker panel accents. In 1972, GS monograms were used on the fenders and deck, and large dual exhausts and functioning hood scoops were installed.

Bench seats were standard, buckets optional on all models. Do not mistake the California GS, a 1968 with Gran Sport trim but the baseline Special 250 V-8, for a true Gran Sport.

Performance and utility

Red-hot as usual, the 400 and 455 engined cars provided six-second 0-60 mph sprints, but little else in the way of performance, being limited at the top end, nose heavy and too stiffly suspended for all-around grand touring. The quality of fit and finish was indifferent. These cars were heavy on gas, especially the big-blocks. They had room for four, but more than that would be cramped. Overall dimensions were reasonable.

Problem areas

Bear in mind that emission controls arrived in 1968, and kept getting stricter as time went on. Muscle cars suffer from control-related drivability problems. In addition, these Buicks were not known for quality of assembly, fit and finish. You can spend a great deal more than it's worth making a Gran Sport better than the factory delivered it. (See also Problem areas in Chapter 19.)

Summary and prospects

Much of what was said about the earlier Gran Sport (see Chapter 18) applies to these last-gasp Buick muscle cars. Like most cars of their age, they were aimed at a market that had dropped out of sight, partly through changing interests, partly through the cataclysm of the Vietnam War.

Convertibles command quite impressive prices today, but the closed models tend to

Last of the breed, the 1972 Gran Sport had a modified hood with functional scoops, which wrapped down more in the front to give the car a lower appearance. The vinyl top was a typical option but doesn't do much for the car's overall lines. Try to find one with the monotone paint job, without vinyl.

be dirt cheap, and will not appreciate rapidly. The production figures are particularly worth considering; some of these cars were extremely scarce even when new. A good clean original, a convertible especially, represents a nice find.

Production

	1968	1969	1970	1971	1972
GS350 hardtop	8,317	4,933	9,948	—	—
GS400 convertible	2,454	1,776	—	—	—
GS400 hardtop	10,743	6,356	—	—	—
GS455 convertible	—	—	1,416	—	—
GS455 hardtop	—	—	8,732	—	—
Gran Sport hardtop	—	—	—	8,268	7,723
Gran Sport convertible	—	—	—	902	852

1968-72 Gran Sport

Engine

Type ..... eight-cylinder V-type, water-cooled, cast-iron block and heads

Bore and stroke .... 4.19x3.64 in. (1968-69 GS340), 3.80x3.85 in. (1970-72 GS350), 4.04x3.90 in. (1968-69 GS400), 4.31x3.90 in. (1970-72 GS455)

Displacement .... 340 ci (1968-69 GS340), 350 ci (1970-72 GS350), 399.7 ci (1968-69 GS400), 455 ci (1970-72 GS455)

Valve operation .... overhead

Compression ratio 8.5:1 (1971-72 GS350, GS455), 10:1 (1970 GS455), 10.25:1 (1968-69 GS340, 1970 GS350), 11:1 (1968-69 GS400)

Carburetion 4-bbl

Brake horsepower .. 260 gross @ 4200 rpm (1971 GS350), 280 gross @ 4600 rpm (1968-69 GS340), 315 gross @ 4800 rpm (1970 GS350), 315 gross @ 4600 rpm (1971 GS350), 340 gross @ 5000 rpm std. (1968-69 GS400), 345 gross @ 4800 rpm opt. (1968-69 GS400), 360 gross @ 4600 rpm (1970 GS455), 175 net @ 4200 rpm (1972 GS350), 225 net @ 4600 rpm (1972 GS455), 270 net @ 4600 rpm opt. (1972 GS455)

Chassis and drivetrain

Transmission ...... three-speed; four-speed auto. opt.; Hurst shifters opt. on several models

Rear axle ratio .... 2.93:1-4.30:1 (varied with trans.)

Front suspension .... independent, coil springs, tube shocks

Rear suspension ..... live axle, coil springs, tube shocks

Dimensions and weight

Wheelbase .... 112 in.

Overall length .... 202 in. (1968-69), 200 in. (1970-72)

Track .... 58 in. front, 59 in. rear

Tire size 7.75x14 (G78x14)

Curb weight .... 3375-3600 lb.

Performance

Acceleration ... 0-60 mph: 8-10 seconds (GS340, GS350), 6-8 seconds (GS400, GS455)

Top speed .... approx. 110-115 mph

Fuel mileage .... 11-14 mpg

1968-70 Riviera

History

A facelift in the purest sense of the word, the 1968 Riviera looked much heavier, thanks to its new combination bumper and grille, and bumper and taillight. A more ornate version of this theme appeared in 1969, but the 1970 frontispiece was more conventional. Throughout this period, the Riviera shell was essentially unaltered, its wheelbase remaining 119 inches, although the facelifts did add inches to the overall length (compare specifications here with those in Chapter 20).

Buick was responding to the numerous federal mandates that arrived in 1968. The new car had a padded dash, roller switches instead of knobs or toggles, side-marker lights (cleverly doubling as a badge at the rear) and so on. It was all very dull going, and collectors have predictably not re-

The 1968 Riviera's best angle is this one, because the front end was considerably hammed up while the rear was characteristically clean. Note the use of rear fender marker lights, which double as badges. Drivability was just as good as in 1967, and handling is generally thought to have improved.

The 1970 Riviera received a hulkier look through the use of rear fender skirts, and the grille was improved. An interesting touch was the body color molding edged in thin brightmetal.

sponded as well to this era Riviera as to its forebears.

Mechanically, however, these cars were steadily improved. A relocated Panhard rod helped give more precise handling in 1968. (The Gran Sport version so impressed road tester Tom McCahill that he pronounced it the best 1968 he had tested—but Tom was given to hyperbole.) Handling improved again in 1969, with revised suspension geometry and stiffer springs and shocks, and from this year on variable-ratio power steering was standard. For 1970, Buick introduced its new, "sanitized" 455 V-8 engine, which had important improvements to valvetrain oiling and a more efficient rocker arm assembly—as well as an astonishing 510 lb-ft of torque at a low 2800 rpm.

Identification

All three years continued with the 1966-67 body shell. The 1968-69 models, however, carried a huge combination bumper and grille encompassing the parking lights, and the taillights were integrated with the rear bumper. In 1968, the cars had upright center hood molding, a plain grille mesh, oblong front marker lamps and separate back-up lamps. In 1969, they had flat center hood molding; three horizontal chrome ribs in the grille; smaller, nearly square front marker lamps; and back-up lamps in the taillamp clusters. In 1970, they used a vertical-bar grille bisected by a center bumper, and exposed quad headlamps.

Performance and utility

These Rivieras remained big, comfortable, long-distance road cars as in past years, but were more sophisticated mechanically and handled better. Depending on what was ordered, they could also be quite a bit faster. The extra performance was achieved by a dealer-installed Stage 1 camshaft kit (1968-69), and a Stage 1 factory kit including a hotter cam, recalibrated carb, performance manifold and heads, oversize intake and exhaust valves, revised distributor and valvetrain, and Stage 1 emblems. The Turbo 400, a smooth new automatic with altitude compensation, replaced the Turbo Hydra-matic 400. Buick's new Controlled Combustion System (CCS) heated the carburetor when cold (mainly to help lower exhaust pollutants).

Problem areas

The 1968-69 430 engined cars continued to suffer from poor valvetrain oiling and resultant engine damage. This was cured with the 1970 455, which had a revised rocker arm assembly and oiled the valvetrain through the lifters and pushrods instead of through the blocks and heads. Engine repairs are expensive on all big-engined Buicks, so if you have any doubt about a car, seek the opinion of a competent mechanic.

Rust is a problem on all three models, and all cars should be carefully checked, especially in the trunk floor, inner fenders and rocker panels.

Calipers and rotors should be checked for wear and corrosion on cars equipped with the desirable front disc brakes.

Summary and prospects

If the 1966-67 Riviera tops out at $7,000 for a mint Gran Sport, the 1968-69 has said it all, in terms of price, at perhaps $4,500—and most of them sell for less than that (one price guide won't go higher than $3,500 for the finest 1968). The 1970 model is harder to peg: mechanically it was the best Riviera yet, but in terms of style it was the most conventional. Since styling has always been the first criterion of collectors, values for 1970s tend to be ten to twenty percent below those for comparable 1968-69s. All three models are unlikely to rise in value as rapidly as earlier Rivieras; conversely, they are good buys for the limited purse.

Rivieras are complicated cars. A mint, low-mileage 1970 stands to cause you much less grief than a well-used 1966, despite the classic styling of the 1966.

Production

	1968	1969	1970
Riviera	49,284	52,872*	37,336

The 1969 was the highest-production Riviera in history.

1968-70 Riviera

Engine
Type . . . . . eight-cylinder V-type, water-cooled, cast-iron block and heads
Bore and stroke . . . . 4.19x3.90 in., 4.31x3.90 in. (1970)
Displacement . . . . 430 ci, 455 ci (1970)
Valve operation . . . . overhead
Compression ratio 10.5:1, 10:1 (1970)
Carburetion . . . . 4-bbl downdraft
Brake horsepower . . . . 360 gross @ 5000 rpm, 370 gross @ 4600 rpm (1970)
Chassis and drivetrain
Transmission . . . . Turbo 400 auto.
Rear axle ratio . . . . 3.07:1, 2.78:1 std. (1970); others opt. (1970)

Chassis and drivetrain
Front suspension . . . . independent, coil springs, tube shocks
Rear suspension . . . . . live axle, coil springs, tube shocks
Dimensions and weight
Wheelbase . . . . 119 in.
Overall length . . . . 215.5 in., 217.4 in. (1970)
Track . . . . 63.5 in. front, 63 in. rear
Tire size and type . . . . 8.55x15, H78-15 (1970), radials opt.
Curb weight . . . . 4360 lb. (1968), 4327 lb. (1969), 4342 lb. (1970)
Performance
Acceleration . . . . 0-60 mph: 8-9 seconds
Top speed . . . . 132 mph
Fuel mileage . . . . 10-13 mpg

1970 Electra 225 Custom convertible

History

Although the 1970 Electra 225 was not much changed from the 1969, the convertible model had the honor of being the last really huge Buick softtop. Its dimensions were colossal: 127 inches of wheelbase, nearly nineteen feet in length, nearly two tons in weight. Yet it was cleanly styled, capable of a turn of speed, plush and comfortable for six full-size passengers. These characteristics, plus its end-of-an-era status, give it above-average collectibility among seventies Buicks, at least for those who like their cars big.

Strictly a facelift model, the 1970 Electra had a new grille but carried the usual four

The first or last of any model is always of interest to collectors. The 1970 Electra 225 Custom convertible was the last really huge Buick ragtop, smoothly styled and very luxurious.

By this time the combination bumper-grille dominated the design of all Buicks. *1970 Buick Division catalog*

111

ventiports on its front fenders. Its great length was emphasized by a full-length brightmetal strip along the lower body, carrying right on through its standard fender skirts.

The convertible came only in custom trim, with a full array of standard luxury touches such as clock, full carpeting, leather and vinyl upholstery, and a battery of courtesy lights. Standard too was Buick's new 455 ci V-8. The convertible sold for only $4,802 base, but traffic, smog and the universality of air conditioning worked against it, and only about 6,000 were sold.

Identification

A boldly textured grille was set into a large full-perimeter bumper surround. Grillework consisted of five rows of four oblongs on each side of the center division. The body creaseline flowed upward from the rear fender, wrapping around the front wheelwells.

Performance and utility

Fast enough in a straight line but, as you might expect, a handful on any twisty road, the Electra was built for long-haul highway cruising, where it is at its best. Road testers said it would do 120 mph, with 0-60 mph times in the twelve-second range. Despite the huge engine, it is tractable at around-town speeds, although a monster to park and navigate. Quality control was indifferent.

Problem areas

Rust and corrosion are significant threats to the 1970 Electras, and potential purchases should be carefully inspected. Because Electras were complicated cars, and even this convertible is not a high-return investment, collectors should be chary about acquiring anything less than a mint low-mileage un-restored example. (See also notes under Problem areas in Chapter 22.)

Summary and prospects

Since the world will never see cars this big again, jumbo convertibles ought to enjoy steady value appreciation in the years ahead, provided they are clean originals. As with other one- or two-star Buick collectibles, it is possible to sink more money into a restoration than you will ever get out. Current top values for a near-perfect, low-mileage example are running at $6,000 to $7,500; be extremely wary about investing more than that.

Production

	1970
Electra 225 Custom convertible	6,045

1970 Electra 225 Custom convertible
Engine
Type ..... eight-cylinder V-type, water-cooled, cast-iron block and heads
Bore and stroke .... 4.31x3.90 in.
Displacement .... 455 ci
Valve operation .... overhead
Compression ratio 10:1
Carburetion .... 4-bbl downdraft
Brake horsepower .... 370 gross @ 4600 rpm
Chassis and drivetrain
Transmission .... Turbo 400 auto.
Rear axle ratio 2.56:1
Front suspension .... independent, coil springs, tube shocks
Rear suspension ..... live axle, coil springs, tube shocks
Dimensions and weight
Wheelbase .... 127 in.
Overall length .... 225.8 in.
Track .... 63.4 in. front, 63 in. rear
Tire size and type H78-15
Curb weight .... 4341 lb.
Performance
Acceleration .... 0-60 mph: 12 seconds
Top speed .... approx. 120 mph
Fuel mileage .... 9-12 mpg

Chapter 24

1971-73 Riviera

History

The number of stars assigned on this one is purely arbitrary, and more of a median than a precise rating. You either love the boattail Riviera or you loathe it—and I side with Bill Mitchell, who conceived of it.

From the sixties through the eighties, it was extremely difficult to create really unique designs in Detroit, yet Mitchell suc-ceeded again and again—with the 1963 Riviera and Corvette Sting Ray, the 1965 Corvair, the 1966 Riviera, the post-1980 Cadillac Sevilles and the Riviera boattail. Mitchell put together the talented crew that designed these cars, and gave it inspiration.

The 1963 and 1966 Rivieras were the work of Dave Holls, himself a car collector; the 1971 was done by Jerry Hirshberg. Both

Buick styling floored everybody with the third-generation Riviera, announced for 1971. Another car mightily influenced by GM's chief of design Bill Mitchell, this Riviera had classic overtones with its radical boattail rear and prominent rear wheel arches, from which a tra-ditional-style sweepspear jutted rakishly for-ward. The detail work was good: side-marker lights were neatly integrated and the front bum-per mirrored the nerf style that had originated with the first Riviera eight years before. Don't buy one with a vinyl top; there's plenty going on with this design as it is.

Wild rear-end styling is plainly seen on this 1972 Riviera, which can be told from its predecessor by the lack of trunk louvers and, up front, the use of an egg-crate-style grille. Buyer reaction was reasonably enthusiastic: sales held at the 33,000 level for the duration of this body style, which was toned down considerably the following year.

stylists point out that Mitchell was heavily involved and that he "wanted a classic." Hirshberg admitted to writer Larry Gustin that the boattail Riviera "looked slightly eccentric. But so would a Corvette if it were the size of a Cadillac." (Like the classic 1963 Sting Ray, the Riviera had its rakish lines complemented by a twin-dash interior.)

Even Mitchell admits that the design was contrived, and that it aged badly in facelifts. "It got so wide," he says, "a speedboat became a tugboat." But nobody will mistake

This factory photograph is included to show what a mess the optional bumper guards make of an interesting design on the 1973 Riviera. The guards were not mandatory, as the following photos reveal. For 1973, Riviera had a horizontal-bar grille and a much more conventional deck. Vinyl was still available for the top.

This well-maintained 1973 Riviera Gran Sport is owned by Thomas H. Smith of Corte Madera, California. Repainted but otherwise original, the car shows 85,000 miles. *Bud Juneau*

In 1973, styling changed dramatically out back, where a conventional (regulation) bumper replaced the pointed 1971-72 unit, though body shape remained mainly as it had been. This was a design compromise, and among fanciers of these Rivieras the 1973 is a shade less desirable.

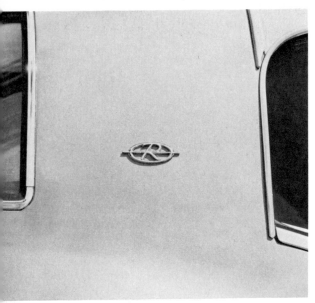

it for anything else on the road. Furthermore, big as it was, the boattail was a splendid performer. Disc front brakes were now standard, and the Gran Sport Stage 1 option gave 345 hp (270 net), with appropriate performance.

Identification

Unmistakable boattail rear body styling appeared on all three models, but the tail was broadened on the 1973. In 1971, the cars displayed trunk louvers, the rear license plate offset to the left, a grille with multiple thin horizontal bars and oblong parking lamps in the lower bumper. In 1972, they had no trunk louvers, the rear license plate offset to the left, egg-crate grillework, black rub strips on the bumpers and parking lamps as in 1971. In 1973, the rear license plate was centered, the boattail disappeared on the deck, the bumper was a conventional full-width design with back-up lamps inset below and separate from the taillamp clusters, the grille comprised four prominent horizontal bars, parking lamps appeared in the fenders outboard of headlamps and massive 5 mph bumpers extended from the body.

Performance and utility

These Rivieras were excellent performers—and the last that were. In 1974, the Riviera lost not only its distinctive styling but its horsepower rating, as the 455 was

These badges are from Smith's 1973: the GS (Gran Sport) label appeared under the name on the fenders, the decade-old Riviera logo was used on the roof quarters and the Stage 1 badge was mounted on the grille. The Stage 1 badge means . . .

. . . 260 hp from the specially modified 455 V-8 under the hood. This figure indicates net brake horsepower, which is around 350 gross bhp. Compression was unchanged at 8.5:1, so the Stage 1 might just accept a tankful of regular now and then—but premium is recommended. *Bud Juneau*

Mag-style chromed wheels were a nice feature on these Rivieras, giving a light look to the styling although they were not as light in weight as they might appear. The Riviera monogram badge was retained in the hub centers, but knock-offs had been declared hazardous to one's health. *Bud Juneau.*

Quartz halogens would have blended nicely with the wrapped parking and cornering lamps, but the United States was still in the age of Neanderthals lightswise. Brightmetal surrounds are subject to a lot of road abuse, and replacements are hard to find. *Bud Juneau*

The Skyhawk for 1976 dropped the Italianate B-pillar for something more conventional to GM: a blacked-out window frame, white-letter tires and tape strip decoration. Turbo-blade 1975 wheels were also dropped.

models) that multiple clones for many divisions is a bad idea, but this is a lesson Buick is still learning.

The Skyhawk was designed to be an affordable sporty car, and until technology passed it by, it did achieve this goal. Its Buick parentage gave it the fine V-6 engine, which Buick had dramatically re-acquired from AMC during the 1973-74 fuel crunch—but in Skyhawk guise it proved a mixed blessing. As much as people admired its pretty lines, they could not find anything the Skyhawk

This is the 1978 version with its ugly egg-crate grille, done in body color rather than blacked out. The result is not entrancing. Few other changes occurred, and the mag-style wheels had been unaltered since 1976. Sales had bottomed in 1977 but improved to an all-time record in 1978.

For 1979, stylists improved the Skyhawk package considerably, louvering the trailing end of the side windows and applying a fine mesh grille. Wheels were also restyled, and a spoiler was another new feature. This shape was retained through the end of production.

did really well: performance was modest, gas mileage unexceptional, the interior cramped, the workmanship indifferent.

The Skyhawk is included here for oddity value—and because the odd one is being collected. But in many ways it was a non-Buick, alien to traditional concepts, foreign to Buick collectors.

Identification

This was a fastback coupe with a prominent B-pillar. Model years may be told by grille variations. In 1975, the grille was a blank oblong. In 1976, the grille was the same except that three stripes at the top ran onto the hood. In 1977, an egg-crate design was used with a nameplate above the grille to the right. In 1978, an egg-crate design was used with a nameplate above the grille to the left. In 1979, a fine-mesh egg-crate design appeared. In 1980, the grille was blacked out with a thin horizontal dividing bar.

A variation that adds to a Skyhawk's value was the Road Hawk option package available in 1979-80. It included flashy exterior tape stripes and paint scheme, Road Hawk decals, a rear deck spoiler, mag-style wheels, a wraparound front spoiler and oversize radial tires, but no extra power under the hood.

Performance and utility

The V-6 provides a good combination of performance and economy, but it also lightens the front end on this car, which allows dramatic oversteer that is all too easily induced, scaring the bejabbers out of the inexperienced, who may find themselves going sideways, or backwards. Brakes on 1975 and early 1976 models were inadequate, fading and smoking after a couple of hard applications. Again, there's no room in the back for anything save luggage and two midgets with pipe-stem legs. Decent fuel mileage can be obtained if you're careful, but no amount of lead in your foot will give a really jolting takeoff.

Problem areas

Rust is the first, second and third most important thing to worry about on the Skyhawk, which was derived from the Monza, which was derived from the Vega . . . need I say more? Poor quality control means a lot of make-work projects to tidy up the factory's flubs. On manual cars, look out for slipping clutches after years of life with careless drivers; on automatics, look for slipping bands and leaks. The engine itself is a sturdy, reliable unit.

Summary and prospects

Chevy's Monza has a fair collector following, but the Skyhawk is nowhere with Buick fans. That's probably because Buick people demand different traits in their automobiles. As a Buick, therefore, the Skyhawk makes a great Chevy.

Still, if you need something small and efficient for running around town, and don't expect it to be anything more than a sporty two-seater, the Skyhawk might be a practical addition to your stable. Do not spend more than $3,000 for one, however; by 1995 it will probably be worth that same $3,000, plus inflation. And at $3,000, it had better be ninety-five percent perfect.

1975-80 Skyhawk	
Engine	
Type	six-cylinder V-type, water-cooled, cast-iron block and heads
Bore and stroke	3.80x3.40 in.
Displacement	231.0 ci
Valve operation	overhead
Compression ratio	8:1
Carburetion	2-bbl downdraft
Brake horsepower	110 net @ 4000 rpm (1976, 1980), 105 net @ 4000 rpm (1977-78), 115 net @ 4200 rpm (1979)
Chassis and drivetrain	
Transmission	five-speed (1976), four-speed (1977-80); auto. opt.
Rear axle ratio	2.56:1, 2.96:1 opt.
Front suspension	independent, coil springs, tube shocks
Rear suspension	live axle, coil springs, tube shocks
Dimensions and weight	
Wheelbase	97 in.
Overall length	179.3 in.
Track	54.7 in. front, 53.6 in. rear
Tire size and type	BR78-13 radials
Curb weight	2750-2850 lb.
Performance	
Acceleration	0-60 mph: 13.5-15 seconds
Top speed	approx. 100 mph
Fuel mileage	20-24 mpg

Production

	1975	1976	1977	1978	1979	1980
Skyhawk	29,448	15,768	12,345	24,589	23,139	8,322

The final-year 1980 Skyhawk was generally unaltered from the 1979 Skyhawk—still a clunky little beast, held by many to be a non-Buick. One in factory-fresh condition should cost no more than $3,000 today.

1974-78 Riviera

History

Whether the 1974-78 Rivieras should be included here is doubtful. That they are is perhaps due mostly to the Riviera's past. Once "big, flashy, fast and unique" (to borrow *Road Test*'s line), in 1974-76 the Riviera was simply big, and as for the downsized 1977-78 series, most people would mistake it for a workaday two-door sedan.

What, then, are their saving graces? Luxury, smoothness and comfort—right up there with the Cadillac-Lincoln brigade—for the 1974-76 generation; a certain tautness and efficiency for the 1977-78s. GM did a marvelous job with the 1977-78s, reducing them by six inches in wheelbase and an astonishing 750 pounds in weight. Nevertheless, it offered only the 350 engine as standard, and an optional 403.

That probably leaves you as unimpressed as it does me. But if you want a plush-lined four-seater (forget about three-across seat-

Whether it was still a Riviera or just a dolled-up two-door sedan is a good question; the 1974 Riviera departed from past radicalism and wasn't even a true pillarless hardtop. Contrary to popular belief, this kind of styling resulted more from production economies and a new approach to hardtops than from fear of federal rollover standards (although the latter could not be discounted completely since these 1974s were designed around 1971).

127

Shown here is the massive 1975 Riviera, a land yacht announced by battering-ram 5 mph bumpers with built-in bumper guards. Note the moon roof. The grille was now composed of thin vertical bars. It is difficult to look at these cars as lineal descendants of the novel 1963-73 Rivieras.

ing, and two people are cramped in the back), a super clean, low-mileage post-1973 Riviera won't cost you a king's ransom.

Identification

The boattail design was completely eliminated. In 1974, a wide, vertical-bar grille appeared. In 1975, thin vertical bars replaced the wider bars and smooth-finish wheel covers were used. In 1976, identification was similar to that in 1975, with revised turbine-style wheel covers. In 1977, the cars were downsized by half a foot, with a near-square grille composed of eighteen vertical teeth containing smaller vertical blades and with parking lenses moved from the fenders to under the headlamps. In 1978, identification was similar to that in 1977, with a

This is the last behemoth Riviera, the 1976 with the S/R performance package. Expect under 15 mpg fuel economy and, for its size, not a lot of room in the back. Things were going to get better, however.

less ornate, vertical-bar grille and oblong instead of square cornering-marker lights on the front fenders.

Performance and utility

The 1974-76 cars were sluggish beasts, doing 0-60 mph in twelve to thirteen seconds while returning 13 to 15 mpg economy. The much lighter 1977-78 is a better choice if you want to enjoy driving: 0-60 mph times are in the nine- to ten-second range despite its smaller engines, although fuel economy is not much better. Both generations suffer from quality problems, and—despite their size—both are mainly two-seaters with room in the back for an occasional two more.

Problem areas

Tractability problems occur through 1976, but the 350 cars of 1977-78 were better sorted out. Rust can be counted on

in areas with severe winters—but one would not want a less-than-superb example of these Rivieras.

Summary and prospects

These Rivieras are to the earlier models as the post-1967 Corvette is to the original Sting Ray, or the Mustang II is to the original Mustang: they will rise in value only after their predecessors rise, and probably not as much. Since the prices for 1971-73 Rivieras are depressed, and even prices asked for 1963-67 models are comparatively low, you cannot hope for much upward movement among the 1974-78 crowd.

The best argument in favor of owning one of these cars is personal preference, or the chance encounter with an extremely clean example. But note the opinion of enthusiast Craig N. Parslow of Calgary, Alberta, Canada: "I would not recommend the 1974-76 Riviera as collectible. It is ugly as sin."

Downsized six inches and lighter by 750 pounds, the 1977 Riviera was a far more nimble car than its late predecessors—but still merely a luxury two-door sedan whose main claim was its nameplate. Save for mint originals with incredibly low odometer readings, these Rivieras are not likely to do anything among collectors.

Riviera carried on in downsized form for several years before being completely redesigned and revitalized. Production reflected its lack of originality: while earlier Rivieras had scored over 30,000 per year, by 1978 these cars were down around the 20,000 mark. Wire wheels and a Mitchell-style paint job add interest to this 1978 two-door sedan.

Production

	1974	1975	1976	1977	1978
Riviera	20,129	17,306	20,082	26,138	20,535

1974-78 Riviera

Engine

Type ..... eight-cylinder V-type, water-cooled, cast-iron block and heads
Bore and stroke .... 4.31x3.90 in. (1974-76), 3.88x3.53 in. (1977-78), 4.35x3.38 in. opt. (1977-78)
Displacement .... 455 ci, 350 ci (1977-78), 403 ci opt. (1977-78)
Valve operation .... overhead
Compression ratio 8.5:1 (1974), 7.9:1 (1975-78)
Carburetion .... 4-bbl downdraft
Brake horsepower .... 210 net @ 4200 rpm (1974), 205 net @ 3800 rpm (1975-76), 245 net @ 3800 rpm (1975-76 Gran Sport), 155 net @ 3400 rpm (1977-88), 170 net @ 3400 rpm (1977-78 Calif.), 185 net @ 3600 rpm (403, 1977-78)

Chassis and drivetrain

Transmission .... Turbo 400 auto.
Rear axle ratio .... 2.93:1 (1974-75), 3.23:1 (1974-75 Gran Sport), 2.56:1 (1976), 2.41:1 std. (1977-78)

Dimensions and weight

Front suspension .... independent, coil springs, tube shocks
Rear suspension ..... live axle, coil springs, tube shocks

Dimensions and weight

Wheelbase .... 122 in. (1974-76), 119 in. (1977-78)
Overall length .... 226.4 in. (1974), 223 in. (1975-76), 218.2 in. (1977-78)
Track ... 63.5 in. front, 63 in. rear (1974-76); 62.2 in. front, 60.7 in. rear (1977-78)
Tire size and type .... JR78-15 radials: (1974-76), GR78-15 radials (1977-78)
Curb weight .... 4732 lb. (1974), 4680 lb. (1975-76), 3785 lb. (1977), 3701 lb. (1978)

Performance

Acceleration .... 0-60 mph: 11-12 seconds (1974-76), 9-10 seconds (1977-78)
Top speed .... approx. 110 mph
Fuel mileage .. 10-13 mpg (1974-76), 11-14 mpg (1977-78)

1978-81 Regal Turbo sport coupe

History

Buick invented the modern ohv V-6 back in 1962, opted out of it in 1967, and bought it back in 1974. But it wasn't until 1978 that engineers decided to give it serious performance, through the popular and efficient turbocharger.

The 231 V-6 of the seventies was considerably modified from its sixties form. The original ninety-degree cylinder timing configuration had been changed to an even-firing 120 degrees, with appropriate changes to the camshaft and 120 degree spacing for the distributor timing. The turbo was the

Crisply styled and quick, the 1978 Regal Turbo sport coupe was a performance package in the current idiom: compact, pillared and powered by a good six. Aside from their good performance, these cars were markedly well built, with doors that close solidly and controls that don't fall off in your hands.

icing on this improved cake: with the two-barrel carb it raised brake horsepower from 105 to 150 and torque from 185 to 245 lb-ft. The four-barrel option gave 165 bhp and 265 lb-ft.

At the same time, the 1978 Regal was cut loose from the Century, downsized and sharply restyled, to do battle with personal coupes like the Cougar XR7 and Chrysler Cordoba. It lost 560 pounds and a foot of length in the process, but good design produced more room inside, a larger trunk and a flat floor. The 1979 was mildly restyled with improvements to engine breathing, and V-8s (non-turbo) became optional. Power steering, automatic transmission and power brakes were standardized in 1980, and a big styling change arrived in 1981. The Regal Turbo coupe now received a chiseled, wind-cheating body, which rode on standard low-roll-resistance radials.

Regals in general sold well, but the Turbo coupe was a peripheral product. Its resulting rarity, combined with its technical interest and (at least in 1981) exceptional styling, place it among the "possibles" for future collectibility.

Identification

These cars carried Regal identification throughout. In 1978, they had turbo-type wheels. In 1979, they displayed large oblong cornering lamps in the front fenders and multispoke wheels. In 1980, they used four rectangular headlights and a coarser vertical-bar grille texture. In 1981, they had a more sloping, aerodynamic nose and a higher rear deck.

Performance and utility

The enthusiast-oriented Gran Touring suspension package was a sport coupe standard that gave this car better-than-average roadholding. Do not expect the usual combination of economical-normal-running and performance-on-demand that more sophisticated turbos usually offer. The blown V-6 is a fine performer, but fuel mileage is no better than with an unblown 305 V-8. Fit and finish are above average: more glitzy than on an Olds Cutlass, less so than on a Pontiac Grand Prix, which shared the body.

Problem areas

Turbochargers are subject to abuse by the ignorant. They ought to be free-wheeled at

The Regal Limited coupe for 1979 is shown here. Note how, on this and the 1978 version, stylists gave the wheel arches added emphasis, in a design reminiscent of the original Olds Toronado. Compare this vinyl top treatment with that of the cleaner 1978 and 1980 in this chapter.

idle after a long, hard run before the engine is shut down, and frequent oil changes are needed to preserve their working lives. Unfortunately, American drivers are not prone to do either of these tasks—so the prospective purchase should be gone over carefully by a qualified Buick service department. (The cars are young enough that you can find people around who understand them.) Rust remains a problem on these intermediates. Interior finish was well done and materials seem to last.

Summary and prospects

With Buicks of the eighties, predicting their ultimate collector status is difficult. The Regal Turbo coupe is a car with great character, however; it has technical interest and high performance, and it was well built for its time. Nevertheless, it does not pay to sink a lot of funds into returning one to like-new condition. As with many other Buicks of this period, pay what is asked for the exceptional low-mileage car, and you will spend less in the long run.

Production

Buick has not broken out Turbo coupe production from total Regal volume, which ran between 200,000 and 300,00 per year.

Still, the Turbo's share is certainly not more than ten percent, or 20,000 to 30,000.

1978-81 Regal Turbo sport coupe

Engine

Type	eight-cylinder V-type, water-cooled, cast-iron block and heads
Bore and stroke	3.80x3.40 in.
Displacement	231.0 ci
Valve operation	overhead
Compression ratio	8:1
Carburetion	2-bbl downdraft, 4-bbl opt.
Brake horsepower	150 net @ 3800 rpm, 165 net @ 3800 rpm (4-bbl), 175 net @ 3800 rpm (1979), 170 net @ 3800 rpm (1980-81)

Chassis and drivetrain

Transmission	three-speed auto. std.
Rear axle ratio	2.93:1 std.
Front suspension	independent, coil springs, tube shocks and antiroll bar
Rear suspension	four-link live axle, control arms, coil springs, tube shocks

Dimensions and weight

Wheelbase	108.1 in.
Overall length	200 in.
Track	58.5 in. front, 57.7 in. rear
Tire size and type	P195/75R-14 radials
Curb weight	3153 lb. (1978), 3190 lb. (1979-81)

Performance

Acceleration	0-60 mph: 10-11 seconds
Top speed	approx. 110 mph
Fuel mileage	16-20 mpg

Buick did little serious facelifting in this period, and the 1980 Regal looked almost identical to the 1978 (the front sidelamps changed from vertical to horizontal in 1979). Note that these factory photos are not necessarily all of turbocharged cars; there was no exterior difference among cars powered by different packages.

1982-85 Riviera convertible

History

With all the hullabaloo caused by Lee Iacocca's revived Chrysler convertibles in 1982, relatively few noticed that Buick too had a ragtop—the first since 1975. It was offered in white or Firemist red, replete with a full complement of goodies: four-speed overdrive automatic; full independent suspension; four-wheel disc brakes; power steering, brakes, windows, door locks, seats and radio antenna; locking wire wheel covers; factory air conditioning; cruise control; and red leather upholstery. Options included digital instruments and Premium

This factory photo shows the first Riviera convertible, the 1982. Elegant and up-to-date, this ragtop was converted from the coupe for Buick by Cars and Concepts. (Cars and Concepts had also handled softtop conversions for Dodge and Chrysler.) Unfortunately, the topless Riviera cost a cool $10,000 more than the coupe, which kept production low—and helped its status as a collectible later.

Is the Riviera in this factory photo a 1983, or a 1982? You will need to look at the car's VIN to correctly identify this as a 1983 Riviera. The year 1983 represented the zenith for Riviera convertible sales at 1,750 units. Most of those who now own convertibles are holding onto them.

Sound (a fifty-watt, four-speaker audio system designed to broadcast to a one-mile radius when you lowered the top).

Like all the ragtop revivals in 1982, the Riviera convertible was a conversion job. It was designed and built by American Sun Roof in Lansing, using half-finished Rivieras from the Linden, New Jersey, assembly line, shipped topless to Michigan.

Buick buyers paled when they saw the softtop's $25,000-plus price tag, a cool $10,000 higher than that of the Riviera

A slick new waterfall grille arrived for the 1984 Riviera convertible, but it was just a little too reminiscent of the Chrysler version. Aside from paint and trim there were no other physical changes. A very few of these 1984s were built with turbo V-6s, but best performance comes from V-8 models.

coupe. Fewer than 4,000 were built over four years of availability, when dealers could barely give them away. Buick had hoped to offer this model as a less-expensive, buy-American alternative to the Mercedes 380SL; instead, customers decided that the alternative was a Chrysler or Dodge convertible. The result: instant rarity. The model year production figures are enough to make a collector's mouth water.

Posh and a little pretentious, hailed as an American Rolls-Royce by coiners of hyperbole, the Riviera was heavy and therefore sluggish with the V-6, but handled remarkably well. A desirable permutation was the S-type (later renamed the T-type), with sport suspension and turbo V-6, as well as less glitzy body trim. All these Rivieras wore the crisp GM E-body, which looked pretty grim on the closed Riviera but somehow just right on the convertible.

In today's aerodynamic world, the 1982-85 Riviera convertible may seem old and blunt and obsolete. But so do a lot of very desirable collector cars.

Identification

In 1982, black bumper rub strips were used for the first time on this series Riviera. The 1983 was virtually identical, an extension of 1982 production, which started late; check the VIN (vehicle identification number). For 1984, the egg-crate grille was replaced by a fine vertical-bar affair. There was little change on the 1985.

Vehicle identification numbers for all years are as follows:

This factory photo shows the final, 1985 Riviera convertible, of which only 400 were built. Consult VIN suffixes to tell this from a 1984 model. The Riviera softtop's perennial problem was its high price, and this also works against its immediate value as a collector car. The same amount of money is better invested in a convertible from the 1950s or 1960s, which will sell at around the same level and rise much faster in value.

136

Year	Model	VIN suffix
1982	Z67	CE400001-up
1983	Z67	DE400001-up
1984	Z67	EE400001-up
1985	EZ67	FE400001-up

Performance and utility

Performance is poor with the V-6, better with the S-type or T-type turbo (1984-85), best overall with the V-8. Roadholding is uniformly good. Rear visibility is limited and passenger space is cramped, as is cargo capacity.

Making this car into a convertible involved less shoring-up than with a unibody platform; extra cowl fender bracing, extra gussets in the rear wheelhouses and wedges that allowed the doors to contribute to rigidity were all it took. The result was a remarkably solid car compared with ragtops of the past, and one that was also quiet for an open car. Rear seat room is severely limited owing to the space taken up by the top well.

Problem areas

These are complex cars with a reputation for high maintenance costs. They are still young enough that most examples will have a traceable service record at a Buick dealership, and this record should be consulted. A built-in problem area is the high-geared Turbo Hydra-matic—set for economy rather than for such a heavy luxury car—but there's nothing you can do about it, except to be sure you find one with the V-8 or the scarce turbo V-6.

Summary and prospects

This Riviera will definitely be a collector car of the future. It had average annual production under 1,000; it is well made and good looking; it comes in flashy colors with a leather interior—and its top goes down.

Initial used-car value guides showed average retail prices depreciating a whopping $10,000 in the first year, and the cars are so recent that prices haven't yet bottomed. Dealers know about these things, however, so the odds that you can find a really nice one for $15,000 are not good, and not improving. Your $15,000 would probably be better invested in, say, a 1949 Riviera (a car

with proven pedigree and many admirers), but you would tend not to drive and use a 1949 as you would a 1985.

Production	1982	1983	1984	1985
Riviera convertible				
V-8	1,141	1,622	442	351
V-6	107	128		
3.8 turbo V-6			11	
4.1 V-6			47	
white	898	1,114	280	150
red	350	636	220	250

Note: *3,556 with V-8, 246 with 4.1 V-6, 96 with 3.8 turbo V-6; 2,442 white, 1,456 red, plus 96 turbos (no records match colors and engines, so I can't say how many turbos were white; some were red in 1985)*

1982-85 Riviera convertible

Engine

Type . . . . . . six-cylinder V-type, water-cooled, cast-iron block and heads (std. through 1984, opt. late 1984 and 1985); Olds-built cast-iron V-8 (opt. through 1984, std. late 1984 and 1985); turbocharged V-6 (opt. 1984-85)

Bore and stroke . . . . 3.97x3.40 in. (V-6), 3.80x3.39 in. (V-8), 3.80x3.40 in. (turbo V-6)

Displacement . . . . 252 ci (V-6), 307 ci (V-8), 231 ci (turbo V-6)

Valve operation . . . . overhead

Compression ratio 8:1

Induction . . . . 4-bbl downdraft, port fuel injection (1984-85 turbo V-6)

Brake horsepower . . . . 125 net @ 4000 rpm (V-6), 140 net @ 3600 rpm (V-8), 190 net @ 4000 rpm (turbo V-6)

Chassis and drivetrain (front-wheel drive)

Transmission . . . . four-speed overdrive auto.

Final drive ratio . . . . 3.15:1 (V-6), 2.73:1 (V-8), 3.36:1 (turbo V-6, 1984 Calif. V-6)

Front suspension . . . . independent, torsion bars, wishbones, tube shocks and antiroll bar

Rear suspension . . . . . . independent, semi-trailing arms, coil springs, antiroll bar, tube shocks, electronic level control

Dimensions and weight

Wheelbase . . . . 114 in.

Overall length . . . . 206.6 in.

Track . . . . 59.3 in. front, 60 in. rear

Tire size and type . . . . P205/75R-15 radials

Curb weight . . . . 3750 lb. (1982-83), 3786 lb. (1984), 3977 lb. (1985)

Performance

Acceleration . . . . 0-60 mph: 18-19 seconds (V-6), 12-13 seconds (V-8)

Top speed . . . . approx. 100 mph (V-6), approx. 105 mph (V-8)

Fuel mileage . . . . 14-18 mpg (V-6), 12-16 mpg (V-8)

137

Chapter 30

1982, 1984-87 Regal Grand National

History

Prowlers of NASCAR (National Association for Stock Car Auto Racing) circuits in the early eighties understood why Buick built the Grand National. Buicks were just better wind cheaters than anything else around; the drivers loved them. So Buick spun off the NASCAR publicity and introduced the incredibly limited production (215!) Grand National at Daytona in 1982. It looked great with silver-gray and charcoal paint and red striping, T-roof, cloth-and-leather buckets and sharp alloy wheels, but it was a toothless wonder: power came from the 4.1 liter V-6 with an anemic 125 hp.

So Buick scrubbed the Grand National for a year, coming back in 1984 with a potent, turbocharged, Turbo Port Injection, 200

Despite a paint stripe package that made it look like a true screamer, the 1982 Regal Grand National could barely outrun a Volkswagen with its V-6—but people snapped up the 215 built, and are still looking hard for them today. Buick produced no Grand Nationals in 1983.

After learning a thing or two, Buick brought the Grand National back for 1984 with more serious all-black paint, new alloy wheels, Turbo Port Injection and enough volume to meet the antici- pated high demand. These Grand Nationals could run with the best of the 1984 fleet. The package remained pretty much static in succeeding years.

hp V-6. This engine powered the Grand National through final production in December 1987 (no 1988 models were officially offered). From mid-1987, the Grand National was the only rear-drive Regal in the line, and had even more power. The 1984-87s were distinguished by all-black paint jobs, a dearth of body ornamentation and good-

Brightmetal blades in the black grille distinguish the 1985 Regal Grand National, which was a carryover project from 1984. Buick built about 6,000—and wished it had built more, as demand was strong. Demand for this car has not slacked off much today.

Recognition points on the 1986 Grand National are its three faint horizontal bars behind a mesh grille, and redesigned wheels. Plainly visible is the fender badge containing name and turbo graphics, common to Grand Nationals since 1984.

looking Lear-Siegler bucket seats. There was less nonsense about them—and a lot more excitement behind their wheels.

The ultimate Grand National was the GNX, with engine, body and suspension modifications by McLaren Engines, teamed with ASC Inc. (formerly American Sun Roof). Despite this outside influence, the GNX was a commemorative car conceived by Buick Chief Engineer Dave Sharpe, who wanted to see off the last rear-drive Regals in style. The specifications included a specially improved intercooler, plus a new transmission oil cooler, a ceramic turbine and dynamic oil seal in the turbocharger, and a recalibrated computer monitoring system. The drivetrain modifications comprised a modified rear suspension with Panhard rod and longitudinal torque bar; sixteen-inch aluminum wheels shod with Eagle GTs, poking out of the oversize, flared fenders; analog instruments; and front fender air exhausts—"Portholes!" as Larry Gustin and Terry Dunham wrote in their latest edition of *The Buick*. Yes, in a way, the beloved portholes had returned.

Identification

In 1982, these cars had a distinctive silver-gray and charcoal two-tone paint scheme with red accents.

Later models can be distinguished by their slightly different grilles. In 1984, they had all-black grilles with fine vertical bars. In 1985, the grilles used six bright accents. In 1986, a fine multi-bar vertical grille appeared with three thin horizontal bars behind. In 1987, thicker grille teeth were set wider apart and a Buick nameplate was offset to the left.

GNX models carried a GNX badge above the Buick name on the grille.

Performance and utility

The 1982 model was a sheep in wolf's clothing. The 1984-87 Grand Nationals were tire smokers, and the GNX improved on them by a quantum leap: *Car and Driver* reported a 0-60 mph time of 4.7 seconds with the GNX prototype, which was probably in the ballpark (although you have to take what *Car and Driver*'s staff says with a grain of salt; they also claimed 4.9 seconds for the standard Grand National!). A fair summary would be that the Grand National is rear drive, rides hard, has no room in the back and lays rubber in all the gears. They just don't build cars like that anymore.

Problem areas

The chief pitfall with any muscle car is its past life; these cars tended to be used hard,

The last Grand National was the 1987 model, built through the end of the year as the sole remaining rear-drive Buick in the line. A total of 8,000 were built. When Grand National production finally finished up, a long tradition ended—and left a lot of hungry customers. "People would call us begging to put it back into production," recalls Buick public relations manager Larry Gustin. But the end had come.

The 1987 Grand National GNX was signified by a GNX badge above the Buick nameplate on the grille. Note the functional air exhausts on the front fender, jumbo 16 inch aluminum wheels, low-profile Eagle GT tires and flared fenders. This is clearly the most desirable of the Grand National tribe—but only 500 were built.

although the many investors who bought new GNXs may have left most of them in great condition. Cars should be carefully checked for rust, and the entire drivetrain should be looked at by an expert. Attempt to obtain service records, which should be available, at least on the later models. (See also notes under Problem areas in Chapter 31.)

Summary and prospects

The GNX was announced with a sticker price of $29,290 by the aftermarket suppliers—who wholesaled the run of 500 cars to the dealers, who in turn bumped the prices up considerably. Demand was triple or quadruple supply, but as often happens with made-to-order collectibles, it tailed off after the initial hype, and a GNX probably cannot command that much right now. There is no doubt that it will quickly surpass original list in the immediate future, however, as will the better-preserved examples of the standard Grand National. This includes the 1982 model, despite its gutless-wonder aspects, simply because it is so rare and so good looking. It is hazardous to make predictions for cars this young, but all the usual factors favor high collectibility, except that they aren't convertibles.

Production

Production of the 1982 was 215 units. Buick built about 5,000 to 8,000 Grand Nationals each year from 1984 through 1987.

The 1987 model year extended through December 1987 and saw 8,000 Grand Nationals in all, of which 500 were converted to GNX specifications.

1982, 1984-88 Regal Grand National
Engine
Type . . . . V-6 cast-iron (turbocharged from 1984)
Bore and stroke . . . . . . 3.80x3.40 in., 3.97x3.40 in. (1982)
Displacement . . . . 231 ci, 252 ci (1982)
Valve operation . . . . overhead
Compression ratio 8:1
Induction . . . . . port fuel injection, 4-bbl downdraft (1982)
Brake horsepower . . . . 125 net @ 4000 rpm (1982), 200 net @ 4000 rpm (1984-86), 245 net @ 4400 rpm (1987), 300+ net (1987 GNX)
Chassis and drivetrain (front-wheel drive)
Transmission . . . . four-speed auto. overdrive, three-speed auto. (1982)
Final drive ratio 3.42:1, 2.41:1 (1982)
Front suspension . . . independent, wishbones, heavy-duty coil springs, tube shocks and stabilizer bar
Rear suspension . . . . . . rigid axle, four links, heavy-duty coil springs, stabilizer bar; modified with longitudinal torque bar and Panhard rod (GNX)
Dimensions and weight
Wheelbase . . . . 108.1 in.
Overall length . . . . 200.6 in.
Track . . . . 58.5 in. front, 57.7 in. rear
Tire size and type P215/65R-15, P195/75R-14 (1982)
Curb weight . . . . 3200 lb.
Performance
Acceleration . . . . 0-60 mph: 15-16 seconds (1982), 7-9 seconds (1984-87), 4.7 seconds reported by *Car and Driver* for 1987 GNX
Top speed . . . . . approx. 115-120 mph, approx. 105 mph (1982)
Fuel mileage . . . . 15-20 mpg, 17-22 mpg (1982)

1986 LeSabre Grand National

History

Unlike the Regal Grand National, the LeSabre Grand National was created especially for stock car racers. To qualify as stock with NASCAR, Buick had to build 100 copies. It built a few more than that, although how many actually made the street is debatable.

Like the Regal Grand National, the LeSabre version came initially in solid black (white was considered but not built), equipped as standard with the taut sport suspension and

Similar in design concept to the Grand National, but built purposely to help hot Regals qualify as stock for NASCAR racing, the LeSabre Grand National saw only 117 copies. If you encounter one, you can recognize it from its blanked-off rear quarter lights. An all-black paint job was standard.

Eagle GT tires on fifteen-inch alloy wheels, and powered by the SFI 3.8 liter V-6. A leather-wrapped steering wheel and blind rear quarters were also standard.

Identification

Unmistakable closed rear quarters, an all-black paint job and Grand National badging distinguished these cars.

Performance and utility

Buick's full-size family car was redesigned this year, gaining front-wheel drive and losing twenty-two inches of length along with 400 pounds. The Grand National's complement of Grand Touring suspension, 3.8 V-6 and oversize Eagle GT tires makes it a capable performer on all types of roads and quick off the line. Nevertheless, the car's NASCAR intent did not affect tractability: It is smooth and pleasant to drive even at low speeds.

Problem areas

"I work on warranty matters," says Buick owner Jil McIntosh of Oshawa, Ontario, Canada, "and my desk drawer is full of fuel injectors that fail on cars less than a week old. My bench downstairs is littered with computers in the same condition. While problems with these parts can be solved now—expensively—what will happen in ten or fifteen years? The various Grand Nationals I'd like to buy as future collectibles, except for two things. The first is money. The second is life-expectancy of all the fancy goodies."

Cars should be checked carefully for signs of hard use and wear throughout the drivetrain, and given the usual examination for rust, although at this writing it would be early to expect to find any.

Summary and prospects

Lots of cars as rare as the LeSabre Grand National have never taken off in the collector market, so don't be overly influenced by the stunning low production figure. It is far too early to assess the LeSabre Grand National's ultimate standing, but there is plenty of interest in the Regal Grand National, so this class of Buick already has a following. My best guess at the moment is that this car is a strong candidate for rapid appreciation.

Production

	1986
LeSabre Grand National	117

1986 LeSabre Grand National

Engine
Type ...... six-cylinder V-type, water-cooled, cast-iron block and heads
Bore and stroke .... 3.80x3.40 in.
Displacement .... 231 ci
Valve operation .... overhead
Compression ratio 8:1
Induction .... port fuel injection
Brake horsepower .... 200 net @ 4000 rpm
Chassis and drivetrain (front-wheel drive)
Transmission .... four-speed auto. overdrive
Final drive ratio 3.42:1
Front suspension ..... independent, MacPherson struts, lower control arms, barrel springs and stabilizer bar
Rear suspension ..... independent, Chapman struts with lower control arms and stabilizer bar
Dimensions and weight
Wheelbase .... 110.8 in.
Overall length .... 196.2 in.
Track .... 60.3 in. front, 59.8 in. rear
Tire size and type .... P215/65R-15 Eagle GT on alloy wheels
Curb weight .... 3100 lb.
Performance
Acceleration .... 0-60 mph: 8-9 seconds
Top speed .... approx. 120 mph
Fuel mileage .... 15-20 mpg

1986 Century Gran Sport

History

Tradition was served with this notable Century, which packed the kind of premium performance for which its forebears were known from the middle fifties. All 1986 Centurys received a new front end with a slanted grille, new headlamps and restyled side-marker lamps. The base was a T-type

Odds are that the 1986 Century Gran Sport will be a little easier to find than the LeSabre Grand National—but not by much. Production of the Century was 1,029 vehicles, but the car's ordinary origins as a workaday two-door make the ultimate collector value of this Buick hard to judge. Still, it's nice to know that tradition lives on: what better name for a hot standard Buick than Century?

coupe. A solid black color scheme, special fifteen-inch aluminum wheels, a jumbo Buick decal and a spoiler on the deck, and the 231 ci SFI V-6 were standard Gran Sport equipment. According to Gustin and Dunham, the decals could be omitted; if they were, the Buick name did not appear anywhere on the exterior. The Gran Sport was a one-year-only offering.

Identification

A Buick decal was usually found on the rear deck. These cars were sold only in a solid black color scheme, and they had distinctive ten-spoke, fifteen-inch aluminum wheels.

Performance and utility

A particularly fine example of the GM A-body (also including Chevrolet Celebrity, Olds Cutlass Ciera and Pontiac 6000), which itself was considered one of GM's better efforts, this 3.8 liter V-6 with automatic overdrive gives sparkling performance and good handling (at the expense of ride). Tight unibody construction is coupled with good space utilization and better-than-average quality of fit and finish.

Problem areas

The usual warning about some examples having led hard lives applies. (See also Chapter 31.)

Summary and prospects

Production figures are low enough to get collectors interested, but it is early to make any serious predictions. The Century Gran Sport uses a plebian two-door sedan body style; whether this can be overcome by its special mechanical and physical details is not known. An exceptionally nice, low-mileage example is worth owning, if you can get it at a decent price.

Production

	1986
Century Gran Sport	1,029

1986 Century Gran Sport

Engine
Type ...... six-cylinder V-type, water-cooled, cast-iron block and heads
Bore and stroke .... 3.80x3.40 in.
Displacement .... 231 ci
Valve operation .... overhead
Compression ratio 8:1
Induction .... port fuel injection
Brake horsepower .... 200 net @ 4000 rpm
Chassis and drivetrain (front-wheel drive)
Transmission .... four-speed auto. overdrive
Final drive ratio 3.42:1
Front suspension .... independent, heavy-duty MacPherson struts and lower control arms, stabilizer bar
Rear suspension .... beam twist axle with integral stabilizer bar, trailing arms, Panhard rod, heavy-duty coil springs
Dimensions and weight
Wheelbase .... 104.9 in.
Overall length .... 189.1 in.
Track .... 58.7 in. front, 57 in. rear
Tire size and type .... P215/65R-15 Eagle GT on alloy wheels
Curb weight .... 2700 lb.
Performance
Acceleration .... 0-60 mph: 8 seconds
Top speed .... approx. 125 mph
Fuel mileage .... 16-22 mpg

1988- Reatta

History

A sensational new Buick that is on almost everybody's list of the most desirable American cars in current production, the Reatta uses the front-wheel-drive Riviera pan and is Buick's version of the luxury two-seater. It sells for about half the price of the Cadillac Allante, which makes it both a hot property

The Buick Reatta is no Cadillac Allante—and we can be glad of that. The Reatta is a far more advanced, more sporting concept, and it sells for considerably less than the Allante. The hardtop of the present model is not removable, but a convertible Reatta is coming soon (and will be the most collectible body style).

and a potential bestseller. Unlike the Allante, the Reatta is not a convertible—but a ragtop is coming soon.

The Reatta is an honest car, proudly designed by Buick and built at the Reatta Craft Centre in Lansing, Michigan—a crack factory where the workers operate as teams and are proud of what they're doing. Although the V-6 is of familiar dimensions, it has a new counter-rotating balance shaft, and its left and right banks have been re-aligned. As *Road & Track* notes, these modifications made the V-6 "better to suit Buick's split-pin, even-firing crankshaft. The latter . . . is a clever way to make the V-6 forget it's a 90-degree design like its V-8 siblings."

The Reatta comes loaded with antilock brakes, air conditioning, full power (including rearview mirrors), climate control, central locking, cruise control, leather seats, leather steering wheel and theft alarm. The few options include a sunroof and a sixteen-way electrically adjustable driver's seat.

Styling is ninety percent of the battle, and the Reatta looks simply terrific. It should have a great future as Buick's flagship model.

Identification

This model was a close-coupled two-seat coupe with a bubbleback rear window, smoothly integrated glass and taillights, and disappearing headlamps and grilleless air intake under the front bumper. It displayed distinctive yellow, black and chrome circular Reatta badges.

Performance and utility

The Reatta offers an excellent ride, quick-response steering with enough road feel and decent, but not neck-snapping, performance. The classic 0-60 mph sprint takes about nine seconds, which is good but certainly not great. Fuel mileage is not at all spectacular, being well under 20 mpg and a good 5 or 6 mpg less than most testers average with the Allante, a curious irony. The car's full-digital instrumentation is hard to read and, unfortunately, standard.

Road & Track comments again: "The Reatta is supposed to be luxurious, the data panel is high-tech and Buick can't tell one from the other . . . High-tech is when you *cook* great meals because you have a microwave, while

Coming up for 1990, according to Buick: a convertible version of the svelte Reatta, which will certainly become a highly collectible Buick in the years ahead. But it may take several decades for its value to bottom out and start back up again, and the up-front investment will be large.

luxury is when you *eat* great meals because you have a chef." Detroit's insensitivity to automotive aesthetics is notorious, but this is admittedly very critical stuff.

All in all, the Reatta is a nice car, at what passes for a sensible price by today's standards.

Problem areas

It is too soon to say what problems may arise (but see comments in Chapter 31).

Summary and prospects

Prospects depend on just how popular the Reatta becomes. At its price it will never be in the high-volume league, so exclusivity seems assured. The convertible is certain to be more collectible in the long run. Clearly the Reatta is the most exciting and original new Buick since the 1963 Riviera—and we know how collectible that car has become.

Production

From January 1, 1988, to June 4, 1988, 2,488 Reattas were produced.

1988 Reatta

Engine
Type . . . . . . six-cylinder V-type, water-cooled, cast-iron block and heads
Bore and stroke . . . . 3.80x3.40 in.
Displacement . . . . 231 ci (3791 cc)
Valve operation . . . . overhead
Compression ratio 8.5:1
Induction . . . . port fuel injection
Brake horsepower . . . . 165 net @ 4800 rpm
Chassis and drivetrain (front-wheel drive)
Transmission . . . . four-speed auto. overdrive
Final drive ratio 2.97:1
Front suspension . . . . . independent, MacPherson struts, lower control arms, coil springs, tube shocks, antiroll bar
Rear suspension . . . Chapman struts, lower control arms, transverse fiberglass leaf spring, tube shocks, antiroll bar
Dimensions and weight
Wheelbase . . . . 98.5 in.
Overall length . . . . 182.8 in.
Track . . . . 60.3 in. front, 60.3 in. rear
Tire size and type . . . . . P215/65R-15 Eagle GT+4 on alloy wheels
Curb weight . . . . 3380 lb.
Performance
Acceleration . . . . 0-60 mph: 8-9 seconds
Top speed . . . . approx. 125 mph
Fuel mileage . . . . 15-18 mpg

Problem areas for early postwar Buicks

Straight eights

Unlike contemporary Cadillac V-8s, Buick straight eights always start hot—in their day, many people who owned both makes would leave the Cadillac home in warm weather. The straight eight tends to be hard on water pumps, which leak readily; this is not a home project but a send-out-or-replace problem. Heads have soft metal freeze plugs front and rear, and if the rear one loosens you have to pull the head to replace it—so replace it with brass if you ever have the head off.

Carefully check the Roadmaster three-piece exhaust manifold. The center section tends to crack from heat at its junction with the outer sections. Excellent reproduction center sections are available for about $175 from R. B. Boyer, 230 DeGuy Avenue, Hanover, PA 17331.

Sludge in the lower radiator tank can travel into the upper tank and cause cooling problems. Cars should be reverse-flushed and a filter installed ahead of the upper tank outlet.

Early chassis

Buicks of this period—right on through the first V-8s—were noted for howling differentials. Put the window down and listen. Fixing this problem is expensive, and new-old-stock is not available. You may have to buy a parts car, or pirate a quiet differential from a junker, if you can find one.

Full coil suspension means that good shocks are essential. If a car wallows during testing, you will have an expensive overhaul of hydraulic lever shocks ahead; the car's price should reflect this.

Comments from Buick collectors

Collectors themselves selected many of the cars contained in this buyer's guide. I am grateful to all who commented on the preliminary list of collectible postwar Buicks published in my column in *Car Collector*. I was surprised by the broad base of Buick's support. Several letters came on stationery marking the writers as Ferrari people, for example!

Since Buicks appeal to such a wide range of collectors, what they have to say on the subject is of more than passing interest.

My chief advisor was Larry Gustin of Buick Public Relations in Flint, co-author of *The Buick*. "I think *any* Buick from 1946-54 is collectible," Larry wrote, "because all have that big pop-art grille, and from '49 to '54 many models had these highly identifiable design cues—sweepspear, portholes, big hardtop-convertible styling. Though the great grille disappeared in '55, that year Buick was third in sales, setting a record that stood for a couple decades. Even the late '50s cars, especially the chromiest in '58, have collector fans." Larry admits that since he now works for Buick his views are somewhat biased—but who would argue with his assessment? A sparkling clean pre-1955 Buick with that "pop-art" grille never fails to turn heads.

The object of this buyer's guide was to single out the models that are especially collectible. Here are some that Buick fans admire in particular, along with amplifications on some models already included in the book.

1949 Super and Roadmaster sedanets

Don Allen of Winter Haven, Florida, pointed out that I had forgotten the sleek and handsome fastbacks from a pivotal year in postwar styling, 1949. I plugged these beautiful Buicks in without a qualm, alongside the pioneering hardtop Roadmaster Riviera and the 1949 convertibles.

Nineteen forty-nine was a fine year for Buick styling. In 1950, the cars got quite a bit heavier and less distinctive looking, though Don notes that the less ornate 1950-51 Special sedanets deserve honorable mention (before 1950, the Special used prewar bodies).

1950 Special business coupe

Collectors tend to ignore the plebian business coupe, until they hear how rare it is (this happened with the last Packard business coupe of 1951, with its production of a few thousand, which now commands a remarkable value in fine restored condition). Jeff Savage of Watsonville, California, reminded me that the 1950 Special was the last business coupe in the line, with production of only 2,500 units.

Plain-Jane interiors mean a relatively easy job of restoration; exceptional styling means an attractive finished product. You can buy one of these and spend a few dollars on capital improvements, ending up with a drivable and good-looking Buick that doesn't cost a king's ransom—one could call it a poor person's Riviera!

1953 Skylark

Stephen Forristall of Houston, for twenty years a dealer in exotic cars in general and Ferraris in particular, has owned or driven "just about everything" at one time or another, although he just started handling American fifties cars on a limited basis.

"It is here that I became enthralled with my '53 Skylark. It is head and shoulders above the '59 Eldorado Biarritz and '57 Chevy Bel Air convertibles which I owned personally but sold—I would not consider selling the Skylark. It is also much nicer to drive than contemporary Buicks, including the 1954 Skylark. To me, it is possibly the most desirable of all fifties domestics."

1957-58 Century Caballero wagon

Of all the models I did not originally include, this one received the most votes. Hugo de Vries of Ysselstein, the Netherlands (who sent photocopies showing big Buicks still being promoted in the Netherlands in the middle sixties), said the Caballero had "beautiful and successful hardtop styling, based on the Special with the big V-8 engine."

Jeff Savage would extend the nod to the 1958 Century Caballero as well: "The four-door hardtop wagon is a rather rare body style, and these cars are also better equipped than comparable Centurys."

Current values for wagons in ninety-five-point condition are $7,000 for the 1957, $6,000 for the 1958.

1960 Invicta wagon

Here's a real dark horse, also mentioned by Hugo de Vries: "A well-balanced, beautifully styled Buick, which is remarkable for the age of fins; a special wagon with the big 401 ci V-8, probably one of the finest of its kind from the late fifties and early sixties, with a certain elegance which almost all other wagons from this period lack."

I have my doubts. To me it looks like a big lump of iron. No two people ever agree about styling! But note the astonishing production figures: according to the record books, Buick built only 3,471 with two seats, and just 1,605 with three seats—fewer than of the concurrent Invicta convertible. If you want rarity and cargo capacity, one of these in good shape is worth considering.

About $4,500 will buy a nice clean one.

1965 LeSabre Custom 400 convertible

Dr. Christopher Whalley of Edgewood, Maryland, singles out this model as a particularly desirable convertible. This is a crisp, cleanly styled car with the usual convertible scarcity: production was only 6,543, with Buick building 15,000 to 38,000 of the other LeSabres that year. "With the popularity of just about any convertible now, I don't think

A 1960 Buick LeSabre estate wagon.

A 1967 Electra 225 convertible.

that such an inclusion would be out of line," writes Dr. Whalley.

1967 Electra 225 convertible

Jonathan Bogus of Milford, Massachusetts, said this was "one of the most handsome Buicks of the late sixties. Never before or since has such a large car had such beautiful lines. Most cars this size are almost automatically considered to be boxy boats, but this car is a definite exception, a head-turner." Bogus admits he owns one, and has just finished a restoration.

Beauty is forever in the eye of the beholder, and I couldn't bring myself to include *every* convertible, though I did mention the last Electra 225 ragtop, the 1970. I will give an honorable mention to the 1967, which has the added advantage of being built in the last year before Congress got into the car

The 1967 Electra 225 convertible owned by Sheldon MacPherson. *Bud Juneau*

The 1967 Electra 225 convertible owned by John and Charlene Marvin. *Bud Juneau*

design business. A nice one could be quite a sleeper.

1971-75 Centurion and LeSabre convertibles

John T. Immesoete of Chicago said I overlooked these full-size softtops, and they were duly put in: "As the owner of a pristine, low mileage '75 LeSabre, I feel qualified to point out several reasons why these cars are collectible. Most obviously, they are the last big, real convertible Buicks. With all the attention heaped upon the '76 Eldorados, the '75s from other GM divisions are often overlooked, yet they were the last of a breed.

"These Buicks have relatively low production figures. The Centurion in particular represents the end of the big-block, big-

The 1972 Skylark sun coupe.

size American performance convertibles. All offer plenty of luxury, performance, value and styling. I hope and bet this isn't the only letter you receive concerning the gross oversight of these beautiful machines. Any list that includes the likes of the despicable, high-volume 1975-80 Skyhawk, the 1982-85 Riviera 'bastardized sedan' convertibles and the atrocious Regal isn't just incomplete; it's completely skewed."

1972 Skylark sun coupe and 1978 Riviera LXXV

Craig N. Parslow of Calgary, Alberta, Canada, wrote to single out these two special and very limited production trim options. Parslow also mentioned "mid-to-late Centurys with the Free Spirit eagle decal and striping kits. Some of these really stood out from others on the road, especially the 1976 Bicentennial in red, white and blue color scheme." Whether such recent trim options will achieve true collectibility is a question, but they are certainly preferable to the more standardized models from the same years.

1973-75 Regal and Century V-8 colonnade coupes

Dennis Divine of Joplin, Missouri, owns a 1975 Regal coupe, and believes colonnade coupes are underrated. (The term *colonnade* refers to the sweeping B-pillar, which replaced the pillarless hardtop syle in this period.) "Many are V-6 powered, but the V-8s are more desirable," he wrote. "Mine has 100,800 miles on it without being repaired or rebuilt. They ride well and are sturdy. On the minus side, they had a propensity for premature transmission problems, and rust is a constant worry, especially in the rear fenders, door bottoms and back bumper. The rubber bumper impact strip invites hidden rust. Brake and master cylinder troubles crop up, too. But my main problem has been lack of replacement parts, especially plastic. Many interior trim parts are interchangeable with the Olds Cutlass and others, but dash restoration can't be done easily and weatherstripping is forbiddingly expensive. If only repro stuff existed."

1976 Electra 225

I heard from more Canadians than Americans on the merits of Buick's most enormous cars, perhaps because of Canada's vast spaces and wide, straight highways. Jil McIntosh of Oshawa, Ontario, Canada, owns a 1976 Electra 225 Park Avenue: "While it isn't worth anyone's while to restore one, I will look after mine for a long time. I detest small cars! The size of this monster is exactly what I love about it. I'm five feet, four inches, so maybe the psychologists are right." (Absolutely: I am six feet, one inch and haven't driven anything larger than a Saab Turbo since my 1967 Riviera.)

The 1974 Century colonnade coupe.

The 1976 Electra Limited.

"The attention a car this big, in mint condition, receives is unbelievable," Jil continued. "Buick downsized in 1977, and never again will we see a car of that size. Although there are larger cars, the '76 seems to have more heft to it, possibly because of the huge bumpers and big grille . . . While it is a pig in the city, on the highway it's fantastic. A few days after it had received new paint, a new vinyl top and new tires, I was stopped by a man in a parking lot who went on and on about how lovely it was and what good

shape it was in. I broke out laughing, explaining that I was used to getting comments about my '47 Cadillac—this was the first time I had ever been complemented on my 'winter beater'!"

There you are—a recommended sleeper. You read it first here!

1979-85 Riviera

I am wary about recommending any post-1978 Rivieras except convertibles, but Jeff Savage of Watsonville, California, is bullish

The 1978 LXXV Riviera.

The 1979 Riviera.

on the whole span. "These are the first front-wheel-drive Rivieras," he said, "with styling that will remain good looking for decades." Savage said these cars look to him like "a modern Delahaye or late-thirties-style luxury grand tourer." He also thinks they have "far higher resale value than the rather hideous 1986-88 Riviera," which I doubt, the used-car market being overwhelmingly based on age above all other factors. Ultimately, however, he may be right.

1982-85 Riviera convertible
Victor D. Blakely of Topeka, Kansas, would not agree with John T. Immesoete. Blakely wrote to correct me on these cars: "I have a 307 five-liter V-8 in both my '83 and '85 Riviera convertible. They will go from rest to 60 mph in 12.5 seconds. I keep them well tuned, but everything on them is standard. The car you drove that took 19 seconds must have been in awful sick condition." (No—it was a V-6!)

The 1983 Riviera.

Jil McIntosh of Ontario adds, "The Riviera is a lovely car, despite its lack of power. In the ragtop it's especially lovely. A friend has a white-on-white one put away, with 2,000 km on it. It's a garage mate to his 1953 Skylark convertible—a quarter century apart, they're less than fifty numbers apart in production totals."

There seems no doubt that these cars will be among the earliest collectibles from the eighties. "They were distinctive, and rare," said Larry Gustin, mentioning two prime criteria for collectibility. "When they came out they were called the Rolls-Royce of American convertibles. Some day, I think, the '79 to '85 Riv will be considered a modern classic, as will the first Reattas."

Other late models

Larry Gustin mentioned the 1971-72 boattail and the 1973 almost-boattail Rivieras as distinctive cars with an increasing following. My preliminary list included those, but not the low-volume 1986 Century Gran Sport (only about 1,000 built) nor the ultra-rare LeSabre Grand National (117 built). Both are powered by the port-fuel-injection 200 hp V-6, the hottest-performing domestic six since the Pontiac ohc Sprint and the Hudson Hornet.

Maybe not collectible?

Don Allen underscored what I said about the 1975-80 Skyhawk. "You called it a non-Buick. You are so right—maybe non-car would better describe this little pile of junk." I've left it in the book, with but one star, on the grounds that it's different enough to excite some interest, particularly the tape-stripe Road Hawk version.

Allen also suggested discretion when it comes to Roadmaster Rivieras: "I would agree with 1949 and 1951, but not the others, especially the '52 and '53." Not distinctive enough, he thinks. And he can't understand why the 1958 Limited is on the list at all. "Why would anyone want such a hulk?" Maybe for the same reason fifties extroverts wanted Volkswagens.

The 1983 Riviera T-type.

Clubs and specialists

Buick clubs

Car clubs are the lifeblood of the car-collecting avocation, offering concentrated depths of knowledge; sources of expertise and comradeship from people who share your interest; advertising for cars, parts, literature and fads; and, in many cases, highly professional publications. For serious Buick collectors, membership in the Buick Club of America is strongly recommended. For specialists, an array of specific interests are served by the smaller organizations listed here. A stamped, self-addressed large envelope with your inquiry will be appreciated.

Buick Car Club of Australia
PO Box 177
Richmond, Victoria, Australia 3121
   350 members, $16/year

Buick Club of America
PO Box 898
Garden Grove, CA 92642
   5,000 members

Buick Compact Club of America
Route 1, Box 39B
Marion, TX 78124

Buick GS Club of America
1213 Gornto Rd.
Valdosta, GA 31602
   2,000 members, $20/year

Riviera Directory
PO Box 825
Dearborn, MI 48121
   1966-67 models

Riviera Owners Association
PO Box 26344
Lakewood, CO 80226
   1963-73 models, $20/year

Buick specialist vendors

Bob's Automobilia
RD2, Box 137
Annandale, NJ 08801
   Parts, upholstery, accessories through 1953

Buick Nut
Joe Krepps
2486 Pacer La. S.
Cocoa, FL 32926
   New-old-stock and reproduction parts

Buick Specialists
PO Box 5368
Kent, WA 98064
   Parts, 1949-56 models

Buicks Unlimited
19332 Briarwood
Mt. Clemens, MI 48043
   Carburetors through 1970

Classic Buicks
4632 Riverside Dr.
Chino, CA 91710
   Postwar parts through 1973

Dick Garbitt Investment Autos
167 Airport Rd.
Hyannis, MA 02601
   Dealer, Buicks through 1960

Muscle Cars Only
RD1, Box 221
Hunker, PA 15639
   Parts, mid-1960 through mid-1970

Rank & Son Buick
4200 N. Green Bay Ave.
Milwaukee, WI 53209
   Parts, all models

Simmonds Distributing Co.
6120 Elder Creek Rd.
Sacramento, CA 95824
   Body and chrome parts, 1957-69

Robert Wenk
3951 S. Hudson Way
Englewood, CO 80110
   Riviera parts, 1963-65 only

Recommended reading

The Buick: A Complete History by Terry Dunham and Lawrence Gustin

This book won a five-star rating from *Car Collector* when first published. The new edition adds forty-eight pages and has over 800 photos, 100 color plates and a topflight, readable text by Buick experts. This is a model of how marque histories should be done.

Buick Muscle Cars 1965-70 and *Buick Riviera 1963-73*, both edited by R. M. Clarke

Both books consist of reprints, mostly of road tests from popular enthusiast magazines, with 180 photos in each. Very good source books if you don't have the originals.

The Buick Power Book by Martyn L. Schorr

For the money, you can't beat this softbound book if you own a Gran Sport of any kind. It covers models through 1979 with much technical detail, a little history and 100 illustrations.

Buick Riviera 1963-1973 by Chris Wolfe

This book is a first-rate rundown of the most collectible Rivieras by a keen observer of the breed, with 150 detailed black-and-white photos to point out salient features, odd and rare options, and so on. Wolfe sorts out paint and trim combinations, options, year-to-year changes, all in this indispensable softbound book for the true Riviera fanatic. Strongly recommended.

How to Hotrod Your Buick V6

A thick softbound with over 200 illustrations, this is the standard source on do-it-yourself performance modifications for the V-6. Heads, blocks, crankshafts, cams, induction, ignition are all covered. Complete technical data and a list of heavy-duty parts are included.

Muscle Buicks! by Tom Bonsall

A softbound documentary of the high-performance Buicks of the sixties and early seventies, this work is especially strong on Gran Sports. Some reprinted material.

The Buick Free Spirit Power Manual (Covers V-8s from 1961 on.)
Chilton's Buick Century and Regal 1975-85
Chilton's Buick, Oldsmobile, Pontiac 1975-85
Haynes Buick Regal and Century 1974-84
1946-48 Fisher Body Repair Manual
1950-65 General Motors Interchange Manual
1955 Buick Shop Manual
1956 Buick Shop Manual
1966 Chassis Service Manual